PROJECT MANAGEMENT
FOR HUMANS
HELPING PEOPLE GET THINGS DONE

Brett Harned

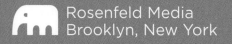
Rosenfeld Media
Brooklyn, New York

Project Management for Humans
Helping People Get Things Done
by Brett Harned

Rosenfeld Media, LLC

540 President Street

Brooklyn, New York

11215 USA

On the web: www.rosenfeldmedia.com

Please send errors to: errata@rosenfeldmedia.com

Publisher: Louis Rosenfeld

Managing Editor: Marta Justak

Illustrations: Deb Aoki

Interior Designer: Danielle Foster

Cover Design: The Heads of State

Indexer: Marilyn Augst

Proofreader: Sue Boshers

ISBN-10: 1-933820-51-9

ISBN-13: 978-1-933820-51-4

LCCN: 2017934297

Printed and bound in the United States of America

HOW TO USE THIS BOOK

Who Should Read This Book?

Project management is not just a role—it's a critical skill that is required in everyday life. Whether you're organizing a party or building a website, you need the skills to complete a task successfully (and we all know that isn't always easy). So this book is not just for project managers, but it's also for people who find themselves in a position where they need to organize and lead projects.

What's in This Book?

The purpose of the book is to provide a solid foundation on leading projects, including the following:

- Information on what project management is and how you can adapt principles and processes to your needs
- Project management techniques to help run projects effectively
- Better ways to communicate and collaborate with multi-functional teams and clients
- Simple techniques for estimating projects
- Ways to build and manage project plans

What Comes with This Book?

This book's companion website (rosenfeldmedia.com/books/project-management-for-humans/) contains a blog and additional content. The book's diagrams and other illustrations are available under a Creative Commons license (when possible) for you to download and include in your own presentations. You can find these on Flickr at www.flickr.com/photos/rosenfeldmedia/sets/.

FREQUENTLY ASKED QUESTIONS

I'm not a project manager. In fact, I know nothing about what project managers do. Can you tell me a little more about it?

The role of a PM can certainly be a mystery—particularly when it's not done well. There are specific characteristics that make a great PM, like being a clear, calm communicator, or adaptable and flexible. And there are a ton of tasks that many PMs take on, such as creating estimates, crafting process, and reporting on project status among others. It's equal parts technical and soft skills. Check out Chapter 1, "You're the PM Now," for the full details on what makes a good project manager.

I keep hearing about Agile, but I can't tell if it's right for me. Is it?

People tend to think that Agile means "fast," but in the context of project management, it's a formal method that is characterized by the division of tasks into short phases of work and frequent iteration and adaptation to meet a goal. It's made up of formalized roles and meetings or "ceremonies" that help guide projects. There is a lot to consider when adopting a new process: project types, goals, budgets, and people. It's best to learn a little about other processes and discuss the pros and cons with your team before just diving in. To learn more about project management methodologies and digital project management principles, check out Chapter 2, "Principles over Process."

I'm terrible at estimating projects. How can I get better?

Hey, creating accurate estimates is tough work. As the word "estimate" implies, there is a lot of guesswork involved. However, if you want to get closer to a really good estimate, you should examine projects or tasks and break them down into subtasks to determine a level of effort. You'll find that information in Chapter 3, "Start with an Estimate."

I'm nervous about talking to my client about how our project is going to be over budget and probably late. Do you have any tips for how I can handle this?

You've got to be comfortable addressing sensitive or difficult issues head on when you're leading projects, because they tend to come up quite often. Whether you're worried about scope creep or you need to address a performance issue with a team member, it's best to take a measured approach that is empathetic and gets straight to the point in order to resolve it quickly. Check out Chapter 9, "Setting and Managing Expectations," to learn about how to set and manage expectations better in order to avoid some of these conversations, and Chapter 8, "Navigating the Dreaded Difficult Conversation," for some tips on how to navigate the conversation itself.

CONTENTS

FOREWORD

After more than 20 years of creating and making things for the internet, I've learned a thing or two. And when it comes to project management, I've found the following to be true:

- **Project management is hard.** Variables like virtual teams, absentee stakeholders, unknown technology, and scope creep can turn seemingly simple projects into mission impossible. Sometimes, it takes every ounce of your energy, patience, discipline, and all the soft skills you can muster to even complete a project, much less make it great or timely.

- **Project managers are routinely underappreciated.** Let's face it—if you're good at your job, your contributions often go unnoticed. And typically, the spotlight is given to other disciplines, like design and development.

I am a designer by trade, but I've often been put into a leadership position. Which means that I've had to practice project management out of necessity, not by choice. Until now, there have been very few resources available to help practitioners like me understand how to manage people and projects. So when Brett told me that he was writing this book, I said, "Take my money!" because *Project Management for Humans* is sorely needed.

Having worked with Brett for the past seven years, I knew firsthand that he'd earned his knowledge the hard way. There's nothing in this book that Brett has not lived through, dealt with, and, at the end of the day, delivered as a project manager.

There are two audiences for this book: the dedicated project manager and everyone else who finds himself or herself tasked with leading projects and teams (designers, developers, strategists, and executives, for example).

For all you project managers out there—whether you're hoping to learn new ideas, change career paths, or validate the hard work that you're already doing—this book provides the advice and ideas you'll need to handle any project situation, no matter how complex.

For the designers and developers who are taking their first steps into project management, you're in good hands. The road ahead will not be easy; pay heed to Brett's advice in the following chapters, and it will help you form great teams and launch successful projects and products.

Finally, a word to the wise: if you are leading projects or teams, seek out the fellowship of your peers. This book is just a start, and it will certainly help you take giant leaps in your career. However, collaborating with your peers will give you even more confidence and enable you to achieve victory often.

Go forth and be great!

—Greg Storey
Austin, Texas
@brilliantcrank

INTRODUCTION

What do you want to be when you grow up?

It's a question we're asked from a very young age. I knew the answer as soon as the question was posed: pediatrician.

I spent the earliest years of my school career preparing myself for medical school, without ever actually thinking about why I wanted that job. When I finally enrolled in college as a pre-med student, I decided to go on rounds with my family doctor just to see what it was all about from the physician's point of view.

Best idea I ever had, hands down.

I won't speak of the things I saw, but I will say that I left the office before lunch and went home to tell my parents it was not the job for me. When they asked, "What is the right job for you?" I had no real response. So, after a year of trying (forcing) biology as a focus, I changed my major to English. I liked writing and thought that would be a good place to start.

When I graduated, I went to the career services office at my university and they handed me a giant book of jobs that English majors might take. That wasn't helpful, so I found my own opportunity at a start-up as an editor. It was a unique role, because I was able to test my strengths: writing copy, managing video shoots, learning HTML and Flash, creating site maps and wireframes, using Photoshop... managing projects. It was an experience I'd never give back, even if I did have to go through the highs and lows of working for a start-up that eventually fizzled out, dashing my dreams of becoming a 22-year-old millionaire.

When I left that job by way of a layoff, I found myself looking for focus. I reflected on what I did best so that I could find the right fit for me. In the end, I recognized that I was:

- Organized
- Curious to learn more

- Willing to help others
- Comfortable asking uncomfortable questions or addressing tricky situations with people and projects
- Courageous
- Detail oriented
- A connector
- A communicator

It took me a few years to find the right fit, but I finally found my calling: project management. For the reasons above, and others to be discussed in this book, I've found that it takes a certain something to be a project manager, and it's partly ingrained in you and partly learned.

NOTE KNOW YOUR STRENGTHS

I've always kept that list of my characteristics in my back pocket, because I knew that it would help me to zero in on what my strengths are as an individual. It has also helped me to assess the "fit" on any potential job and project opportunities. If you're having a hard time figuring out the right role for you, try doing the same and making some connections in your community to help you land in the right role. It'll make you happier.

Project managers reading this excerpt will most likely identify with a similar story. Many PMs—particularly digital project managers—fell into the role with little to no guidance or formal training. Like many before us, we have worked hard to do what feels right in the role, and have adapted systems, processes, frameworks, and guidelines to benefit us, our teams, and our projects. This book embraces that DIY style of project management: being deeply involved, testing ideas and methods, failing, and coming out better. Those are ideals that resonate with anyone in the digital industry. We're still coming up with new ways of working, and we always will, because we innovate.

Whether you accept it or not, you *are* a project manager. Sure, you may identify as a designer, content strategist, developer (or any of the many roles and titles there are in our industry), but as a human being, you are a project manager. Think about the most basic things you do in life, and you can apply project management to all of them: making dinner, moving, applying to college, attending a conference, even a night out with friends or a vacation. You're required to plan, estimate, and communicate. *And it's not that hard.*

This book explores the core functions of project management through the lens of everyday interactions and situations, because there is an aspect of project management in a lot of what we do as humans. The personal stories included in this book are intended for you to have a laugh (sometimes at my expense) and help you draw the connection from daily, nonwork situations to real-life project situations. By calling out these topics in unique, personal scenarios, you'll find that you do not have to hold the title "project manager" to actually be a project manager. In fact, you're likely managing projects—and dealing with a variety of issues—in some way every day. And no matter what you do or whom you work with, if you follow some of the advice herein, you, too, can be a successful project manager.

CHAPTER 1

You're the PM Now

*The heartbreaking truth of being
the project management speaker.*

I had the privilege to speak at Web Design Day, an excellent conference hosted by Val and Jason Head in Pittsburgh, PA, in 2011. Naturally, my topic was project management, and I spoke to a room full of designers and developers…with a project manager (PM) sprinkled in here and there. I knew the room was not full of "my people," and I was excited about it, because I firmly believed that PM skills were necessary for anyone to be successful in project work. I was up for the challenge and willing to take a risk, knowing that I might put some people to sleep. I made my presentation, which covered some PM basics, and was met with a positive response and a good number of questions. It was energizing!

After my session ended, I had a line of people waiting to introduce themselves, start a discussion, or ask a question. I was flattered by this until I spoke to the first person in line, who said, "I've never worked with a *good* project manager."

It was like he had shoved a rusty dagger right into my heart. Really hard. And it hurt!

I recovered quickly, and we talked about the expectations of PMs, how they could help him as a developer, and what their projects together might look like. At the end of the conversation, I decided that maybe the PM in question wasn't that bad. Perhaps the role and the expectations of that PM were never truly set. I offered my advice and asked him to have an honest conversation with his PM about what's needed from his role and how they could partner to make the work stronger.

I like to think that my advice helped and that an unknown, wayward project manager succeeded. I know that the conversation made me even more eager to champion the cause of digital project management and set some standards for the industry.

What Is a Project Manager?

Let's state the obvious here: project managers guide and facilitate projects with a keen sense of budget, scope, timeline, staff, and all of the complicated places in between. No matter where they work, what kind of projects they manage, or what their title is, project managers are the men and women on the front lines of projects, defending their teams, clients, and projects from miscommunication, missed deadlines, scope creep, and any other failures. They champion the well-being of the people involved in their projects and look to make or facilitate strategic decisions that uphold the goals of their projects. That's a hefty job description, and it requires a fine balance of managing the administrative details of a project and its people. While PMs are often lumped in the "behind-the-scenes" aspect of projects, to be highly effective, they need to be part of the bigger strategic project conversations.

PMs are not robots. They are not on your team just to take notes and make sure that you're recording your time properly. Yes, they do work in spreadsheets and follow up on deadlines at possibly annoying rates of speed. But they are not the team's secretary. They are the project facilitator and sometimes the guiding force that makes important conversations, debates, and decisions happen. That means that while managing the operational side of the project, they also must be fully informed on the conversations that are happening on projects so they can drive action in the right direction.

There are so many intangible tasks and qualities of project managers that it's not uncommon for people not to fully understand just what a PM does and if they need one or not. Here's the thing: you always need a PM, no matter what. That PM might be called a producer, account manager, designer, or even developer.

NOTE THE EXPECTATIONS OF THE ROLE

Anyone can be a project manager, as long as that person is clear on the expectations of the role. If you're playing a part-time PM, be sure to discuss what's expected of you in the role and use some of the tactics in this book to guide your PM journey with ease.

The Role vs. the Title

There are many organizations that do not formally employ project managers. In that case, the project team absorbs the role of the PM. So, in this scenario, you'll find a designer or developer leading client communications, project planning, and any other necessary tasks taken on to keep the project rolling. Either way, it's not about a title. It's about the fact that keeping up on the project is a necessity of getting the work done successfully.

No matter where you work, if you're operating projects with deadlines and budgets, you need someone to manage them. It's very possible that your company has a well-established process and employs someone with those three all-important letters at the end of their name, like a PMP® (Project Management Professional) or a CSM (Certified ScrumMaster®). It's also very possible that you have an established process, but don't work with an actual project manager by title. Chances are, you work with someone who handles the PM-like stuff. Maybe she doesn't have the formal title of "project manager," but she's doing the job of a PM, and there is absolutely nothing wrong with that.

> **NOTE** FORMAL PM TITLES AND TERMS
>
> While digital might be new, project management has a rich history that dates back to the creation of the pyramids. Think about it—everything is a project. However, it wasn't until 1969 that the Project Management Institute was formed. Since then, many organizations and practices have been formed to help project managers become better at their jobs. With that recognition came the creation of formal titles, certifications, and many variations of the role itself. If you're looking for more information on the history of PM, check out **www.projectsmart.co.uk/history-of-project-management.php**.

Upon review of those points, you may decide that bringing in a part-time or freelance PM is a better route for you and your company. You can find these people all over the place, as the market for freelance project managers has grown significantly in recent years. Here are some things you might want to consider when bringing a capable PM resource onboard:

- Every company works differently, so be sure to be clear about the expectations of the PM role.

- Get your company's and project's onboarding docs or training together ASAP so that you can feel comfortable that they are fully up to speed on day one for the new hire.

- It takes time to get to know a team and a new company, so be open to this new person and willing to answer as many questions as needed. It will make that person feel more comfortable and successful in the long run.

- Make sure that the rest of your team welcomes the new person (and role) to the team and includes her in the project.

- Introduce this person to your team and your clients in a way that makes her feel included, needed, and a full part of the team. This person will have great responsibility, so you want that to be embraced.

- Provide access to tools, email, meeting spaces, and resources as you would with a full-time employee.

- Have an open door policy so that the PM feels comfortable discussing issues with you.

What matters the most is that you clearly define the expectations of the role before dropping someone into it. Take time to think through what project management means to your organization and then identify the type of person you want to fill that role. That will lead you to success.

The Qualities of Good Project Management

No matter what your background or organizational makeup is, there are certain qualities that you must embrace and principles you should follow to do the job well. Sure, you're going to have to show some interest in creating project plans, estimating projects, keeping the project budget intact, and facilitating great communications, but in order to really do a great job as a project manager, you have to keep your work organized and your teams informed and happy. This can be especially difficult when your budgets are tight, resources are overbooked, and client expectations seem to shift weekly. That's the life of a project manager.

The core competencies of a good project manager are rooted in your ability to navigate rough and still waters with the same level of effort and ease. It's one part technical expertise and three parts emotional intelligence. Consider these core qualities for being a great PM, and check out the PM principles in Chapter 5, "Create a Plan":

- Eagle eye for project issues
- Clear, calm communicator
- Empathetic
- Adaptable and flexible
- Curious
- Invested in the work

Eagle Eye for Project Issues

Each project is unique and comes with its own set of goals, challenges, clients, team members, ideas, conflicts, budgets, and deadlines. That's a whole lot to wrap your head around. Here's the thing: as the PM, you're dropped right in the middle of all of those issues, so you've got to have your finger on the pulse of everything. You're constantly concerned about the well-being of the project and the team, as well as the happiness of the client. Chances are, there's going to be a speed bump or two, and it will be up to you to resolve them. If you're good at what you do, you'll spot those issues before they become big problems and handle them with ease.

Clear, Calm Communicator

Communication is a huge part of project management. Being transparent, direct, and very clear about important project information will make any detail or situation easier to handle. It's also important to let your own style and personality shine through in your communications when the time is right. The best project managers are true chameleons when it comes to communication. They have go-to methods and tools to help facilitate project communications, but when it comes to one-on-one conversations, they adapt to what will help them encourage the team, build relationships, prevent and solve issues, and even share difficult news.

> **NOTE** MORE ON COMMUNICATIONS
>
> Chapter 7, "Communicate Like a Pro," is all about good communication practices. Jump ahead to find better ways to communicate with teams and clients.

Empathetic

Conflict happens, and as a project manager you have to set your emotions aside and do what is best for your project. This means putting yourself in the shoes of the people you're dealing with—whether it's a team member or a client—to understand intent, motivations, and possible outcomes. To truly understand an issue, you have to fully comprehend and understand it, not just listen. In order to do that, you have to understand and dissect what is being said to make sure that you get it. You can't do that without talking to those involved with the sole intent of understanding—and solving—the root cause of the problem. Sometimes, that means you have to be the tough guy and not show any emotion.

Adaptable and Flexible

There's no doubt that projects change from the minute you say "go," and you have to adapt to the change that is thrown at you. This could mean changes in scope, team, and even project goals. Regardless of the change, as the PM you have to find ways to keep a project moving, no matter what. Sometimes, you have to be flexible in your process, about the way you communicate, or even on what your team intended to deliver. Change isn't always easy to accept, but knowing that you can find alternate ways to work and achieve success regardless of its impact will keep you ahead of the game mentally.

Curious

No matter where you work, ideas are flowing and technology is changing. Teams, particularly in the digital space, are collectives of creative minds who come together to meet client goals through design and technology. It's an exciting place to be, and you're going to be constantly challenged with innovative discussions and ideas. Take advantage of the people and resources around you to keep learning and to better your understanding of your industry and how your clients want to leverage your teams' skills. You might do this by reading blogs and books, attending meet-ups and conferences, asking your colleagues questions, or sharing ideas yourself. Additionally, you should do everything you can to understand how other projects within your organization (or even a client's organization) operate. The more you know about operations and similar efforts—and the people involved—the more you will be able to make better project decisions. Lastly, it's important to always be open to learning (and teaching) to keep your skills sharp.

> **NOTE** CONTINUOUS LEARNING
>
> It's not always easy to find great resources to stay abreast with what's happening in project management. Check out this always-updated list of great resources for PMs: **http://brettharned.com/resources/**.

Invested in the Work

This almost goes without saying, but the best project managers are the ones who get out from behind their spreadsheets and play an active role in their projects. Don't just attend meetings and take notes. Participate in them. Hunt down problems and address them. Share your ideas. Share conversations you've had with the team and clients. Shape the path of the project and be the PM who not only cares about what happens internally on the project, but also how your project will succeed when it launches. And, if you are that part-time PM, embrace the role and give it just as much attention as you give your other work. Know that taking on the role of PM doesn't just mean checking off items on a to-do list. It's about thinking critically about the path of the project, its people, and potential outcomes. Keep your eye on project goals and do your best to help the team do the same.

Typical PM Tasks

Again, what you do as a project manager will vary from company to company, but there are some core tasks that will strengthen the perception of your role as a PM. We'll cover these in later chapters, but here's a high-level view of what you should be doing as a PM:

- Create project estimates
- Craft, build, and manage the process
- Create and manage project plans
- Manage tasks
- Report on status
- Plan your team's time
- Motivate teams
- Monitor scope
- Wrangle calendars and meetings
- Facilitate communications
- And much more

Create Project Estimates

Without a basic understanding of what it takes to complete a project, you'll be lost. You should try to gain a general understanding of each person's project role, the effort required, and how that might match up to your project scope and deadline. A great way to do this is by sitting down with people who do jobs that you don't fully understand. Maybe there's a developer or designer on your team who would be willing to walk you through their process to give you a better understanding of the steps they take and the effort associated with each. Once you have a good understanding of that work, you can speak about tasks with confidence and begin to draft estimates.

It can also be very helpful to work with people on your team to create project estimates (see Figure 1.1). This kind of exercise will not only help you create sound estimates for projects, but it also can help you gain a better understanding of different types of work and deliverables, the effort involved, and how they might work together to form a new project process. Plus, you'll come up with a sound estimate that could possibly be reused on similar projects in the future.

FIGURE 1.1

Creating project estimates can be tricky. Work with your team to establish estimating practices that work for you. (Read more in Chapter 3, "Start with an Estimate.")

Craft, Build, and Manage the Process

We all love naming our processes—whether it is an existing term or a newfangled, company-branded one we made up. Either way, you'll find nuances to every team's process, so you can't necessarily just step in and pick something up and expect it to work the same way it did at another company or with another team. You've got to do what you can to understand that terminology, because it will be different from place to place. If you're working in digital, you may run waterfall, Agile, or hybrid processes on your projects. No matter what methodology you follow, you must understand the ins and outs of how your project should run from beginning to end and be willing to help your team through it and spend the time to do it right.

Create and Manage Project Plans

Every project comes with a deadline. It's up to you to understand the process by which your team will meet that deadline and document it in order to keep things on track and communicate progress to others. And guess what? Creating a plan will help you in more ways than one. You can create a line-by-line plan with specific deadlines, a Gantt chart with overall timelines, or even a Kanban board that shows work tasks from initiation to completion (see Figure 1.2). However you choose to handle your plan, be sure to keep the level of time and effort needed to complete the tasks in mind, as well as staffing considerations. There's nothing worse than missing a deadline because you didn't consider the people who would actually be doing the work.

FIGURE 1.2
Project plans can be quick and dirty or complex and measured. Find the right balance for your teams. (Read more in Chapter 5.)

Manage Tasks

You don't want to be seen as a taskmaster or a box checker, but you should always have your finger on the pulse of what's happening on your projects. But how do you keep track of so much at one time? Shared to-do lists and open, regular communication are a start (see Figure 1.3). But also think about routines when it comes to status updates, check-ins, and communications with your team and stakeholders. When you do that, your checking in feels expected and less of a burden and suddenly you become the helpful PM.

FIGURE 1.3
Keeping a master to-do list of all project tasks can help you keep your team and stakeholders on track.

Report on Status

It's the PM's job to keep everyone informed of what is happening—or not happening—on a project at all times. While on-the-go communications are a must, it's important to remember that there's information passed in hallway conversations and even meetings that your whole team might not be privy to. So be sure to keep good notes and be vigilant about keeping your team and clients up-to-date on what's happening on the project on a regular basis. A great way to do this is via status reports that communicate progress, next steps, action items, to-dos, and blockers on a weekly basis. Following these reports up with a phone call to review the items is something that you should also ask for when working with clients. Because let's face it: people just don't read—especially when it doesn't feel urgent. But sometimes your status reports do contain urgent info, and you'll want to talk through it with them anyway. So schedule a weekly call. It will prompt you to write the report and send it, and you won't have to worry about whether or not someone knows what's happening.

> **NOTE** WRITE BRIEF, INFORMATIVE STATUS REPORTS
>
> Status reports keep projects alive! And in order for them to be effective, they need to be brief, readable, and full of relevant information. Learn more about writing great status reports in Chapter 9, "Setting and Managing Expectations."

Plan Your Team's Time

Team staffing can feel like a giant game of *Tetris* when you're working in an organization that handles multiple projects. For example, you work to keep your project moving on a positive path so that you can keep your teams intact for the course of a project, because you know that delays could create gaps in availability for those people who might get pulled onto other projects. As part of a larger PM team, you must work through new assignments and reduce the risk of impacting current assignments by talking through the best-laid staffing plans (see Figure 1.4).

DESIGNER · WEEK OF JAN 12
20 HOURS PROJECT Y
12 HOURS PROJECT Z
8 HOURS ADMIN

DEVELOPER · WEEK OF JAN 12
14 HOURS PROJECT Y
18 HOURS PROJECT Z
8 HOURS ADMIN

FIGURE 1.4

Your team will love you for considering resourcing plans. Learn more about how to create solid staffing plans in Chapter 6, "Managing Resources."

Motivate Teams

Times can get tough on projects: feedback can be brutal, meetings can get tricky, and clients aren't always easy to please. As the PM, you act as the cheerleader and motivator to get your team to do the best job possible (on time and within budget, of course). Whether you pick up pizza for the folks who have to pull an all-nighter or give someone props in front of the entire company for doing a great job, you have to be a motivated PM who is genuine and feels like part of the team. There's nothing more uplifting than being motivated by someone who *actually cares*.

Monitor Scope

Every project comes with some idea of scope and cost, whether that is documented in a formal scope of work or presented to you by a project stakeholder in a meeting. As the PM, it's your job to understand the overall size and shape of the project and to make sure that you stay within those boundaries. In order to do this, you must keep a watchful eye on project requirements, deliverables, and project progress. Perhaps you're watching hours spent in your time-tracking system, or maybe you're keeping an eye on requirements met or goals achieved. Either way, you have to keep a keen eye on making sure that you have quality work, which falls within the scope of what your team has set out to do.

NOTE MORE INFORMATION

Check out Chapter 10, "Scope Is Creepin'," for more tips on managing scope.

Wrangle Calendars and Meetings

Scheduling meetings can be a nightmare, particularly with large groups. As the PM, it's your job to keep an eye on client and team availability and schedule meetings far in advance to ensure that important parties can attend. You should also prepare an agenda in advance of the meeting so that everyone's time is utilized properly. The worst thing you could do is to call a meeting and have no plan for a discussion or a solid outcome. And, when you're in those meetings, you'll want to take good notes to communicate decisions and action items as outcomes of the conversation.

Facilitate Communications

The foundation for healthy projects is built on great communication practices. As the PM, it's your job to make sure that your team and clients are collaborating and communicating about the details. That means playing an active role by setting and managing project expectations, keeping your team communications consistent and transparent about progress and blockers, and sometimes helping your client understand your process, deliverables, milestones, and any other thing that will impact how they experience the project.

And Much More

There's a heck of a lot more that PMs do on a day-to-day basis, but this list covers the most necessary tasks. You may find that you're doing some really basic stuff like ordering lunches (to make everyone happy), scheduling one-on-one check-ins, reminding people to submit timesheets, and other menial tasks. Those are the things that make your life as a PM easier, so kudos to you if you're taking them on.

The PM Is the Backbone

As a PM, it's important to know that you are critical to your team's—and your client's—success. While some of your tasks may seem repetitive and sometimes thankless, know that the team would fall apart without you. And if you're looking to make your job more fun and exciting, do it. How you interact with your team is in your hands, and the more invested you seem to be in your projects, the more your team will trust you to help them and the project.

Embrace the Role

There will be times as a project manager where you contemplate the value of your role, and you might see others doing the same thing. It's easy to do, because the role is varied, and a lot of what you do can go unseen by many. If that is the case, be sure that you're aware of the expectations placed on your role. Are you holding up to that? Then ask yourself a few difficult questions:

- Am I contributing to the project in a positive way?

- Do my team and my clients/stakeholders know what I do with my time?

- How active am I on my projects? Am I watching things happen, or am I driving them forward?

- When was the last time I actually spoke (with words, in-person or by phone) with my team?

If you're a good PM, you are an active member of the collective project team. So, if you are answering these questions and finding that you're really not showing that you are (or want to be) an active part of the team, you're headed down the wrong path. In order to gain any respect, you have to display an investment in your project, or the rest of the team will lose respect for you. You can't just throw a plan together, schedule and check off the to-dos, and call it a day. You must engage in the project and know everything about it and your team.

Stick to Your Guns

Whether you're working with a project manager by title or performing PM-like tasks by role, you've got to know that the tasks are contributing to the success of your project. Define what a PM does at your organization and even spell out how it can be done well. Be open to the conversation and the ideas that your team puts in front of you, and you'll find that both you and your team will be happier. As a result, you will be set up for project management success.

Make Space for Project Management

Usually, you'll find a project manager embedded on a team, or working on several projects, who is responsible for all of the things that make projects profitable and pleasurable, and sometimes more. Full-time PMs are dedicated to their craft and work hard to be a good project manager. But not all organizations employ full-time project managers. That's OK, too. Those organizations may have the skills on staff to ensure that projects run smoothly, or they may experience organizational hiccups (read: missed deadlines, projects going over budget) and recognize that they need some better practices in place around the PM.

Solid PM skills will prove to be valuable in many situations—both personal and professional. Whether you're planning a move or have to estimate a new website redesign project, you'll find that you're doing some level of "PM work." So, if you're reading this thinking "not for me," you're likely wrong. Pick and choose the tasks and values that complement your existing qualities, and apply them. It will strengthen your work overall.

If you find yourself in that situation and still cannot justify hiring a full-time project manager, you can work to sharpen your team's PM skills to help keep their projects on track. Designers, developers, illustrators, strategists, and anyone else on a team can be multitasking PMs on top of their regular jobs. It's just important to keep in mind that adding project management on some folks' plates could make them uncomfortable, especially if it's with a client. Sure, we all manage our own work somehow, but that doesn't mean we're also good at managing other peoples' work, budgets, timelines, and all of the other stuff that goes along with being a PM.

Again, you will need to consider what taking on project management responsibility will mean to you, your clients, and the people who need to make time for it as part of their full-time, non-PM role. Review the qualities and tasks listed earlier and decide which of those translates to project management for your organization. From there, you can think about the qualities that are needed and the type of person you want to fill the role. That will lead you to success not only in matching the role to an individual, but also with matching the role to your organization.

Once you do assign the role, be sure to check in and make sure that your new PM/designer (or whatever other full-time role they hold) is comfortable with the responsibility. It can take a good nine months for a full-time PM to feel comfortable with the job, so you'll want to make sure that you're giving this person enough training and resources as well as time and space to settle in.

by Dave Prior
Agile expert and Certified Scrum Trainer

Nobody really ever wants to be a project manager. If you ask a group of kids what they want to be when they grow up, you might hear things like fire fighter, rock star, Batman...but there is little chance that any of them is going to say, "When I grow up, I want to be held accountable for things I can't control and get blamed for things I was not responsible for." Becoming a PM is not a choice—it is something that happens to you (see Figure 1.5). It can happen for a variety of reasons that all play out across your life like a really slow moving, painfully dysfunctional, superhero origin story. There are some who embrace it with pride and some who spend years trying to pretend it isn't true. Some PMs are driven with a hunger to solve the impossible riddle of finding the "right" way to do it, and some come to terms with the fact that there is no one perfect way to handle all projects.

FIGURE 1.5
The Dark Knight...of Projects. Everything is a project, and he'll save them all.

I've been managing projects for over 20 years and at various points in time, my answer to the question of "What does it mean to be a project manager" has been very different. Early on, I thought it was about managing work, then I thought it was about getting people to do stuff, then I went from following the PMBOK (*A Guide to the Project Management Body of Knowledge*) to abandoning it and "PM" because I wanted to BE AGILE! I spent a lot of time stuck on that last one, hiding in shame at Agile events because I am a PMP. Eventually, I got past that and decided to accept what I am. Agile or not, I am a PM.

I was taught how to be a project manager by a guy named John Dmohowski. He was brought into a web shop I was working at to train me and another guy. He gave us each a book written by Dick Billows and said, "When I'm done with you, everything is a project." I think that may have been the truest thing that anyone has ever said to me. Once someone teaches you to think through things in work breakdown structure, you can't *not* see things that way. It permanently warps the way your brain works. You learn to see things and break them down in a way that normal people can't. And once you learn about risk management, you stop caring whether the glass is half empty or half full. The glass becomes a fragile container of liquid that may fall to the floor, shatter, and cut people so...Band-Aids, we're going to need lots of Band-Aids...just in case.

My favorite example of a project manager was Radar O'Reilly from *M*A*S*H*. Radar always knew what was coming before it happened. He always heard the choppers before anyone else. Everyone took him for granted—until he got sent home and Klinger tried to do his job. It was only in his absence that people understood the true depth of his value. A good PM is like that. If they are doing their job well, it often seems like they aren't really doing anything at all. But take them out of the equation and wheels fall right off the horse.

I'm over 20 years into this job of being a PM. It is my chosen profession and when asked what I do, I usually respond by saying, "I get hit in the stomach with a bag of oranges for a living." (See Uncle Bobo from *The Grifters*.) But now, with all this experience, all this time, all these failures and a few successes, my job is not about a schedule, or deliverables, or risk, or Gantt charts or Burndown charts, status reports, or having a certification...all those things come into play, but they are not what I do. My job is simple and impossible. I love doing it, I am awesome at it, and every day is an adventure in learning how to suck less at it.

I am a project manager. I hack people for a living.

TL; DR (Too Long; Didn't Read)

Solid, practiced project management skills are critical to everyone, whether you're a full-time project manager or absorbing the role for your project team. To fully understand how you can best serve in that role, consider the following guidelines:

- What does the role mean to your team, and what can you do to uphold it?

- How do you look for project risks and act on them with confidence before they become bigger issues?

- How can you be an honest, direct communicator for the sake of your team and clients?

- How can you be open to learning and adapting to people, situations, and projects?

- What does it take to embrace all of the tasks that fall to your role, such as estimating projects, creating plans, managing scope, motivating teams, and so on?

- Can you stick to your guns and do what is best not only for you, but also for the project?

CHAPTER 2

Principles over Process

*There's not a perfect toolkit for any PM or project.
Find the ones that work for you and make your
own masterpiece.*

I'm terrible with directions. Me and any piece of IKEA furniture in a room is a setting for disaster. Anger, curses, quitting. I've always been a fan of doing my own thing, on my own time, my own way. Sure, that sometimes means accepting failure and going back to the directions to do something "the right way," but that's just a part of *my process*. It's the way I have always been.

When I was a child, I would draw for hours. For a long time, I would focus on drawing people—characters I created, people drawn from photos, and even family members. It felt like a natural talent that I was expressing on my own, and I truly enjoyed it. The hobby began to get a little more serious as I got older, and my parents enrolled me in classes. My first life drawing course was eye-opening. I walked in thinking "I got this" and left the first class feeling like I had been doing it wrong all along. The teacher presented a specific way, in steps, that you should draw a body and a face. It wasn't the way I approached it. So I tried the new way, and the outcome was the same.

So what did I do? I decided to use a mash-up of the techniques, and I think that helped me to be better and to hone my own craft.

Most people think project management is just about process or methodology. Those people are wrong. Project management is about so much more: delicately handling communications, having empathy for the people involved in your projects, motivating those people when things go sideways, problem solving, scouting and assessing red flags and making sure they don't become real issues, and above all, providing project leadership that inspires great work and a positive team environment. The methodology is just a part of the PM puzzle, and depending on your project or organization, you'll handle it in a firm or flexible way. That's where formal training can come in handy, because anyone can truly learn and follow a documented process. While it's helpful to have guidelines to keep your projects on the rails, it's even more helpful to follow a core set of principles to keep yourself in check as a project manager.

The World of Project Management Methodologies

Before you go and start outlining your guiding project management principles, it's smart to educate yourself on the many documented project management methodologies. Next, you will find a list of those PM methodologies with basic descriptions. You won't believe just how many there are and how they might not even apply to you. There are plenty of resources for you to dig in, to understand these on a more complex level, but having a high-level understanding of them will help you to understand how you can form your own principles (which we'll spell out later in this chapter).

Traditional Methodologies

If you're a PM purist who needs a checklist and a place for every single project task, you'll love these methodologies. Get excited! Load up that spreadsheet! If that's not quite your thing and you're looking to do something a little "out of the box," you may want to skip this section. Go on, be brave. Either way, check out these basic methodologies that can be used to inform any process—from moving your office or home to building a car, ship, or even a spacecraft!

- **Waterfall:** It's the most widely known PM methodology, which requires one task to be completed before the next one starts (see Figure 2.1). It's easy to plan a project this way, but as soon as change occurs, you'll be faced with scope changes, confusion, and pushed out deadlines. Waterfall is known for the handoff— allowing resources to work in silos. It works in some places, less in others (ahem, digital).

FIGURE 2.1
Everything goes downstream in the waterfall method.

- **Critical Path Method (CPM):** This is a complex method that is actually quite simple! You map out all of the tasks of your project, figure out what needs to be completed before each task starts, and then estimate the time it will take to complete each task. From there, you calculate the longest path of the planned tasks to the end of the project, and you figure out the earliest and latest points each task can start without making the project longer. That's how you determine what's critical and what can be delayed. It's kind of like prioritizing tasks to ensure that you get the most important work done first.

- **Critical Chain Project Management (CCPM):** This methodology focuses most on the constraints put in place by resources (people, equipment, physical space) needed to get the project done. As the PM, you build the plan and identify the tasks that are the highest priority so that you can dedicate your resources to them. Then you place time buffers in your plan to ensure that your resources are available to get the work done. Seems sneaky, huh?

- **Process-Based PM:** This methodology is a little more flexible than the others listed in this section, but a formal process is still required. In general, the difference is that it aligns a project with the company's goals and values. Each project follows these steps:

  - Define the process.

  - Establish metrics.

  - Measure the process.

  - Adjust objectives as needed.

  - Plan improvements and implement them.

NOTE PMI AND PMBOK

While it's more of a set of standards than a formal methodology for managing traditional projects, you should know what it's all about. The Project Management Institute (PMI) created the *Guide to the Project Management Body of Knowledge* (PMBOK), which outlines the following steps for all projects: initiating, planning, executing, controlling, and closing. Check out more at **http://www.pmi.org/**.

Agile Methodologies

Probably the single most buzzworthy project management term, Agile is based on the mindset that self-organizing software development teams can deliver value through iteration and collaboration. It was formally developed in 2001 based on the *Agile Manifesto of Software Development* and is based on a core set of values:

- Individuals and interactions over processes and tools

- Working software over comprehensive documentation

- Customer collaboration over contract negotiation

- Responding to change over following a plan

There's a lot of confusion out there about what "Agile" means, and that might be due to the fact that there are several ways to execute the methodology. Many teams claim they are agile, but they don't use the methodology by the book. That's OK, but that's not Agile with a capital "A." That's just working *faster.* So what is Agile then? It can be boiled down to these main points:

- The product owner sets the project objectives, but the final deliverable can change. (For example, a goal can manifest itself in many ways, and you'll explore them together.)

- The product team works in two-week sprints, which are iterative in nature. At the end of each sprint, the collective team reviews the work done and decides what is complete and what needs iteration.

- Depending on sprint reviews, the final product might be altered to meet the product owner's goals or business needs, and that's OK! (No scope creep here.)

- Everyone collaborates! That's right—open conversations about what works best for the product make for a better final deliverable, and those comments don't just come from developers—they come from the whole team (see Figure 2.2).

NOTE THE *AGILE MANIFESTO*

Written in 2001 by 17 software developers, the *Agile Manifesto* puts forth core values and 12 principles for "uncovering better ways of developing software by doing it and helping others do it." Read the full Manifesto online: **http://agilemanifesto.org/**.

FIGURE 2.2

Plan, iterate, review, iterate, iterate, iterate…review, iterate, deliver, and iterate again. That's the cycle of Agile!

Now that you understand the core of what "Agile" means, you can understand the "flavors" of it:

- **Scrum:** The simplest of Agile methods, because it allows teams to get work done without added complexity that some methodologies introduce. Essentially, the team self-organizes around central roles that suit them: Scrum Master, Product Owner, and Engineering/Development Team. The Scrum Master's role (kind of like the project manager) is to remove any blockers from the team's way in order to get the work in two-week cycles, or "sprints," to get work done quickly. Scrum calls for "ceremonies" (meetings for the uninitiated) to keep things on track:

  - **Daily stand-ups:** A short (15 minutes max) meeting held each day to discuss progress, what's next, and what blockers exist. You stand during this meeting in order to keep it short, because who wants to stand for that long?

  - **Sprint planning:** A creatively named meeting that is a bit longer (an hour max) and comes with the objective plan of what will be done within the sprint.

  - **Sprint review:** A meeting to review all work done at the end of a sprint. In this meeting, you might collect feedback, decide something is done, or decide on an alternate route.

  - **Sprint retrospective:** A meeting held after the sprint review for up to an hour to discuss what might make future sprints more productive.

- **Kanban:** The literal translation of this Japanese word is "signboard" or "billboard." A visual approach to scheduling that aids decision-making concerning what to produce, when to produce it, and how much to produce. It was created for lean manufacturing by an industrial engineer at Toyota. If you've used a tool like Trello, you've used a Kanban board to move tasks through stages to completion on a project (see Figure 2.3).

FIGURE 2.3

Place cards on your Kanban board to track progress. Want an example of a tool that will help with this? Check out Trello, JIRA, or Pivotal Tracker.

- **Extreme Programming (XP):** It's not a part of the X Games, but you might find yourself drinking Mountain Dew while administering this Agile approach intended to improve quality by responding quickly to change. In essence, change can happen within sprints, and teams can change the course of their work being done/planned immediately.

- **Adaptive Project Framework (APF):** This one may resonate for PMs who recognize that you have to adapt your methodology to the project's goals. With APF, you document project requirements, functions, subfunctions, and features before determining project goals. The team then operates in iterative stages rather than sprints, but stakeholders can change the project scope at the start of each stage. So, truly, you adapt to the project and its people.

Change Management Methodologies

Risks are inherent in all projects. You just know something will come up, and you want to prepare for them. These methodologies are meant for PM folks who are hyper-focused on what could pull a project off the rails and subsequently come up with stable ways to get it back under control.

- **Event Chain Methodology (ECM):** If critical path wasn't enough for you, you want to take a look at ECM. The six principles of ECM make up a technique that is focused on identifying risks and their potential effects on a project's schedule. Think of it this way: the ECM PM is living in doomsday. Everything is a risk, and they know how to handle it. On one hand, it makes the team comfortable. On the other, it can be sort of gloomy to always think about the worst that can happen. After all, your control ends somewhere, right?

- **Extreme Project Management (XPM):** Not to be confused with XP or a sick afternoon of Parkour, XPM is all about embracing change and altering project plans, requirements, resources, budgets, and even the final deliverable to meet changing needs. Extreme!

- **PRiSM (Projects Integrating Sustainable Methods):** This methodology for managing change is focused on sustainability, or using existing organizational resources, to reduce negative impact on environmental or social impacts. It follows six principles that are derived from the *UN Global Compact's Ten Principles.* This is serious process work that can make your lives better in major ways.

Other Business Processes, Methods

New ways of working materialize every once in awhile and catch some traction. In fact, one could easily pop up before the publishing of this book, because we're always looking for better ways of working based on what we deliver. While not all of these may really be classified as "methodologies," and they might not apply to you, they are worth mentioning because you might be able to lift an ideal from one methodology to apply it to your own work.

- **Lean:** Do more with less! This methodology is focused on removing unneeded steps, resources, and budgets in order to deliver a product.

If you're in the web world, you've likely heard about applying the Lean methods to user experience work, which has traditionally weighed heavily on project budgets due to an abundance of deliverables (site maps, wireframes, flow diagrams, content inventories, taxonomies, and so many more). Lean UX brings ideas and the actual design of the experience to the forefront of the process, with less emphasis on deliverables. A simple process might look like Figure 2.4.

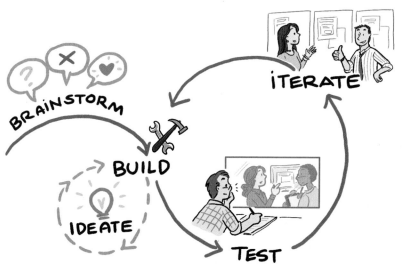

FIGURE 2.4

Brainstorm, build, launch, test, iterate…and keep going until you get it right.

- **Six Sigma:** This is a disciplined, data-driven methodology developed by an engineer at Motorola, and it has been adopted by many large organizations focused on manufacturing. It seeks predictable process results to improve the quality of final products by following a set of steps and removing the cause for defects. A Six Sigma process is one in which 99.99966% of all opportunities to produce some feature are statistically expected to be free of defects. That's quality assurance and profitability!

- **PRINCE2 (PRojects IN Controlled Environments):** This methodology was developed for use by the UK government. The project is tightly controlled and planned before it begins, with stages clearly structured. This process-based approach leaves very little room for questions, as it is based on seven principles, seven roles, and seven process phases with direction on very specific documentation. The role of the PM is a bit different with PRINCE2, as he or she is responsible for basic activities like scheduling, while an appointed project board handles activities like resourcing and goal setting and the team.

- **Benefits Realization:** This methodology's first focus is on the value you deliver to your customers and stakeholders rather than the fact that it was completed. This seems like a core value that should be a part of any project.

Devise a Methodology That Will Work for You

While it's important to have a solid understanding of the many different ways to operate a project, you don't have to feel as though you're tethered to just one way of working, particularly in the digital space. After all, you need to do what works for your team, your clients, and your project. Maybe that means you take a Lean approach to deliverables to meet a smaller budget, or an Agile approach because your team wants to work iteratively and share work rapidly. You get the idea: do what feels right. Don't overthink your process. Try something new, adjust when you see the need, and focus on solid communication and delivering quality work.

If you're having a hard time deciding what steps in a process will work for you, think through these questions and scenarios:

- What is the intended outcome of your project? Is it a product you'll create? An experience? A specific deliverable?

- What are the goals of the project?

- Who needs to be involved in the project based on the answers to the first two questions.?

- How do the people you'd like to assign to the project like to work? Is anyone certified or really, really hard core about sticking to a methodology?

- If you're working with a client, do they subscribe to a methodology? Are you aware of how they work and how their way of working will impact your team?

- Are there any outside factors you need to take into account when planning? (Think about dependencies, project or client values, etc.)

- What is already working for your team? What is working for your clients? Also, what isn't working?

NOTE PMPS, BLACK BELTS, CSMS, OH MY!

Many methodologies come with training and certifications. While they aren't 100% necessary to learn about and administer a methodology, they can be very helpful when trying to understand the foundation of each and deciding what will work for you, your organization, and your projects. So, if you have the resources to be trained and certified, go for it! If you don't, you'll be just fine without those three letters, trust me.

It's amazing what sitting down to think through what the project actually needs versus just doing what you always do can help you accomplish something when searching for alternative ways of working. It will take you no more than 30 minutes to answer all of these questions and come up with an approach that could work for you. Maybe you'll select a single methodology, or maybe you'll try pieces of a couple. Don't get caught up in a "this or that" conversation.

If you're lost and you want some help picking a process, think about it this way: boil the decision down to two very basic principles for understanding all of these methodologies:

- The more traditional methodologies like Waterfall and Critical Path are good for teams who want or require a high level of structure and management. They want tasks spelled out and planned accurately, and a PM who will take control of the details—both for the project and for them.

- The Agile methodologies like Scrum and Kanban are great for teams who are flexible in nature. They prefer a high level of collaboration, are open to change, and are willing to take control of the work and be held accountable for it.

Principles for Digital Project Management

Formalized methodologies are well thought out and considered from the earliest steps to the finalization and wrap-up of projects. When gaps are found on projects, the methodology provides an answer. There are strict guidelines, templates, and microprocesses for administering them, and it's great if you absolutely must follow it by the book, or if you're new to project management. But as you mature as a project manager, you will learn that any old monkey can kick out a templated project plan or report. You'll find a yearning to do more, be more. But what is that? It's furthering your role as a project manager to be an active member of the team who not only facilitates the decisions made on a project, but also contributes to those decisions, provides meaningful input, and keeps a keen eye on where the project is heading.

Project management as a whole is strategic in nature, but many individuals, teams, and companies miss or avoid that aspect of the role. That belittles the role and the value of it, and you end up with that job any old monkey can do. As digital project managers, we're missing critical threads to tie us together and make us stronger professionally—i.e., principles. You see, we're all operating on different planes as digital project managers. We're approaching the job with differences in experience, practice, and attitude. This is to be expected in some ways, but by following a set of principles, you will strengthen the perceptions of the role and show what it means to be a digital PM or even a traditional PM with a renewed sense of value.

The following principles do not suggest that we all operate using a set of the same templates, a single process, or any defined tactics. In fact, that would be horrible, because we need to celebrate the fact that all projects are not created equally. But, operating under the same principles, we create a standard to be used across industries and projects, which will increase effectiveness, help achieve better outcomes, and produce stronger project managers.

1. **We are chaos junkies.**

    We thrive on problems because we know how to solve them. We are highly organized and do everything in our power to maintain order with a calm presence in the face of chaos. When things get out of hand and we can't solve problems on our own, we know whom to pull in at the right moment.

2. **We are multilingual communicators.**

We speak to management, finance, legal, IT, marketing, UX, design, code, content strategy, and more across a wide variety of industries and verticals. We have a broad range of skills and knowledge, and are confident in linking up different perspectives from different specialties using our base communication skills. We work hard to understand the motivations of our teams, stakeholders, and users. We can translate tech-speak to the uninitiated, discuss design without imposing an opinion, and drive conversations to important decisions that will guide our projects to success.

3. **We are lovable hardasses.**

Digital project managers walk the line between servant and leader—caring equally about numbers and people. It's a challenge that requires much thought and consideration about the way we behave. While we are not managers with direct reports, we work hard to build relationships with our team members to serve as confidants, counselors, and friends who have their work and best interests in mind at all times. At the same time, we challenge nonsense when we see it, stand up for our clients and our teams when it's easier to stay quiet, speak up to save our projects, and work darn hard to keep our teams motivated, our clients happy, and our projects on target.

4. **We are consummate learners and teachers.**

Working in an industry that moves so fast, we are inherently adaptable and open to new processes, ideas, practices, and deliverables. We follow what's happening in our industry—from all angles—and do what we can to account for change to make our projects more successful. We're open to bettering ourselves and our peers by sharing our work and practices openly and freely with other DPMs (data protection managers), as well as our team, clients, and stakeholders. We recognize that learning and teaching builds trust in what we do, benefits others, and leads to stronger partnerships and outcomes.

5. **We are laser-focused.**

    We expect change on projects, because we understand that business goals evolve and change, processes fail, stakeholders come and go, and new ideas arise. When asked to change, we use project goals as a basis for discussion on whether or not the change is acceptable. We wade through comments and feedback, and analyze and discuss change to help guide our teams and clients to the best decisions given our focus on project goals.

6. **We are honest, always.**

    Everyone who works with us, clients and partners included, trusts us because they know that we've got their best in mind when guiding process and decisions. We don't cover up mistakes; we illuminate them with the intent of not repeating them. We stay transparent when it comes to scope, budget, and timeline changes. We resolve conflict by remaining neutral and honest about causes and solutions. We truly believe that the truth always prevails, and we champion that in all interactions and communications.

7. **We are pathfinders.**

    We're not box-checkers or micromanagers. We give our teams the agency to create and build without the burden of nagging process overhead. We find new roads to delivery while sticking to principles rather than following the words in a book or training. We forge paths on every project by focusing on the strategic vision first, while having a keen sense of process, timeline, and budget.

These principles apply to anyone who assumes the role of PM or digital PM on a project, and are meant to serve as guideposts for how you conduct yourself in the role. Not every project scenario, issue, or process point is covered in these principles, because the principles will guide your behavior when taking on these challenges. Embrace them. Make them a part of your ethos. Build on them to make them more specific to you. That will make them stronger and more valuable not only to you, but also to the people who have the pleasure of working with you.

TL; DR

Project management isn't just about methodologies or process, it's about people, embracing empathy, communications, problem solving, and so much more. That said, having a firm grip on process, formal methodologies, and principles will help you long-term. Here are some things to consider:

- Exploring and understanding all of the methodologies that exist will help you understand what is possible and what you can adapt in your own project processes.

- It's quite possible that no methodology or process is perfect for you. Use your knowledge to craft one that will work for you and adjust it as you see fit.

- Traditional methodologies like Waterfall and Critical Path are good for teams who want or require a high level of structure and management.

- Agile methodologies like Scrum and Kanban are great for teams who are flexible in nature.

- Using a set of guiding principles for how you behave as a PM can be valuable not only for you and your team, but also for anyone else who takes on the role of a digital PM.

CHAPTER 3

Start with an Estimate

Finding the right estimate for a project can be difficult, especially if there are unknowns.

The roof deck on my South Philadelphia row home has been an issue for us from day one. Every time it rains and the water comes at the house at a very specific angle, we'll get water in the room below. We've had several contractors and roofers visit our house to fix the issue, and every time we're left with a description of work and an estimate for what it will cost, we're completely baffled. One roofer says he'll seal the roof for $500, and it will last us for "a few years" before it needs to be done again, while the next contractor comes in and says "we need to rip it all up and start over" to "find out what's underneath." His estimate starts with a $350 fee to do the demolition, but he doesn't know what he'll charge after that. These are obviously two very different approaches to the same issue with varying costs.

The gaps in approach and cost (or unknown costs) leave us wondering what the best approach is. One roofer can give us a solid estimate because he knows what he'll do and how much of his time and materials it will take to get it done. The other wants to find the bigger problem and isn't comfortable even giving a price range beyond the first set of labor needed to find the problem.

So, if we do decide to rip it up, what will happen if they find something else to fix? The house is a money pit, and we don't want to keep spending money, but it needs to be fixed. We're left questioning the budget and the timeline, but we know we need to do what's best.

. . .

This is a classic case of estimation confusion, and it happens all over the place. The biggest issue is that when we hear "estimate," we suddenly come up with a concrete number or date. But it's just an estimate, which means the number is a best guess (and will very likely change). This happens just as much on digital projects as it does with construction projects, and that's because we're humans and just can't answer unknowns.

Set the Stage for Solid Estimates

No matter what the type, size, or budget of a project is, estimating can be a daunting task. Every project request comes with a set of unknowns, or a gray area that makes a team or individual nervous about expectations concerning cost, timelines, and level of effort. Because the gray area changes from project to project, there is no simple way of saying, "It always takes us this long to do this thing" without qualifying it with some additional factors ("with these people, on this project, in this place, at this time, etc."). It's just not possible to build one solid estimate without doing some investigation of the work at hand. In order to create a workable estimate, you need to know your team, deliverables, tasks, and process like the back of your hand. You also have to be comfortable asking questions to figure out the things that you (and maybe even your potential client or customer) do not know.

You have to be very comfortable with knowing that there are unknowns on your project that might not become apparent until you're really deep in things. At the same time, you must be very confident about the things that you do know, because those things will help you get to the unknowns at the right time—or avoid them with some additional work. A combination of knowing and not knowing details of your project will give you the confidence to come up with an estimate for your project that is workable and possibly even flexible.

> **NOTE** NEVER FORGET
>
> This is the Merriam-Webster definition of estimate. Keep it on hand for when you have to remind someone when your estimate goes off track (because, yes, it most likely will).
>
> ESTIMATE *transitive verb*
>
> **a :** to judge tentatively or approximately the value, worth, or significance of
>
> **b :** to determine roughly the size, extent, or nature of
>
> **c :** to produce a statement of the approximate cost of

Why Estimate?

While building digital products is not the same as building a roof, someone—your team or clients—requires a general understanding of what is needed to get it done successfully. Whether you're working for a client or on an in-house team, you've got to answer to someone who's in need of a project estimate. Sometimes it's hard to understand why that person needs an estimate, so consider these reasons:

- **Estimates are based on a level of effort and times.** Typically, the cost of a project is based on the time spent on a project. Your estimate helps calculate a rough determination of that cost and sometimes whether or not the project is worth the investment.

- **A good estimate will be based on specific tasks and the talent used to complete them.** Your estimate will help you staff the project properly. For example, you can say a senior developer will need four weeks to complete a project, but a junior might need twelve weeks with some support. That's a pretty large detail that will impact your estimate!

- **More complex projects can be dependent on other projects or tasks.** Knowing just how long it will take to complete your project might answer an important question about another project (and when it may have to start or finish).

- **Working with a team can often be a challenge, particularly when no one is in agreement on the project.** Working together to produce an estimate can be a great way to pull the team together to talk about staffing, responsibilities, process, and timing. And guess what, that all helps produce a solid estimate.

It would be very easy, at this point, to just say, *"This is how you create an estimate."* But that wouldn't work in your favor, because there is a mindset that is required to do this the right way—and feel good about it.

Learn What You Can

I work in the web industry, and I'd never sell myself as a web designer or a developer. I'm a project manager. That said, I've learned enough about design and code over the course of my career to make me horribly dangerous. I would never step into a project and say, "I'm the best resource to design or code this," but I know enough about how things are done to ask the right questions and make the proper assumptions about how they *should* or *could* be done. This knowledge helps immensely when estimating project work because I can give a gut check on the level of effort related to any task on a project.

I learned a lot of web skills in my career and have had to stay on top of industry standards and major changes ever since. In addition to that, as a PM, I had to learn a whole new set of people, processes, and clients every time I started a new job with a new company. A career in project management means that you have to stay on top of trends, changes, and deliverables in your industry. It isn't easy, because things change fairly often, but it's worth it because it will directly affect your success as a PM.

There's a lot to be said about what you know at the front end of the project versus what you know downstream. There's this thing that PMs call the cone of uncertainty that is helpful in illustrating the fact that you can only estimate so well up front and your ability to estimate increases as you move through the project. Check it out: **https://en.wikipedia.org/wiki/Cone_of_Uncertainty**.

There's an ongoing, and constantly updated list of resources on my site here: **http://brettharned.com/2013/10/12/stay-informed**. So how do you stay on top of things? Aside from reading relevant trade publications, websites, and blogs and attending training and networking events, you should leverage the people who sit on your team. They are your best asset to stay on top of trends, discuss potential paths and ideas, and create estimates.

Understand the Roles on Your Team

Who the heck are these people on your team and what are they doing all day? Sure, it's easy to read Jim's job description and find out what he "does for a living," but that doesn't tell you much about the mechanics of what he does on a task level. That's what you really need to know. So, how are you supposed to understand Jim's role on the team and how his work will impact an estimate?

You just have to talk to Jim.

One of the best things you can do in your career is to be genuine and honest about what you don't know. If you really want to know how or why someone does his or her job, just ask that person! It might sound silly, but most project managers feel like they're supposed to just know everything. You don't, and that is OK. Remember that it's better to admit what you don't know and ask questions. Doing so gives you an opportunity to connect with your team on an individual level, and it will help you understand the inner workings of your projects. After all, figuring out the steps one person takes to create a deliverable will work wonders in helping you calculate a true estimate.

Of course, every team is different, and there are a lot of teams out there who make do without every single role, but these are the typical roles you might find on a digital design team:

- **Strategist/researcher:** This is the person who spends time at the beginning of the project to understand its users and goals, and who crystallizes its strategic path. This person might conduct research and interviews to get to the root of the goals and how the project might solve the problem at hand.

- **Content strategist:** This person plans for the creation, delivery, and maintenance of content in conjunction with the research and design of a product. This person isn't necessarily the copywriter, although that could be the case on some projects. This person might deliver content analyses, an overall strategy that guides content development, voice and tone guidelines, and more.

- **UX designer:** This is the person who focused on the strategy and the usability, ease of use, and pleasure provided in the interaction between the customer and the product. This person might design site maps, wireframes, or prototypes of the product.

- **Graphic designer:** This person designs the look and feel of the product and provides further input on the design of the UI. This person might deliver style tiles to determine the look and feel of the product, and design full pages or unique parts of the UI in order to create an overall design system for the product.

- **Front-end developer:** This person is responsible for producing HTML, CSS, and JavaScript for a website or web application. It's referred to as "front end" because it's stuff that users see—a design come to life via code. This person might deliver full-page templates or widgets via code.

- **Back-end developer:** This person builds an application (using server-side code like PHP, Ruby, Python, .Net, etc.), which connects with a database (using MySQL, SQL, Access, etc.) to look up, save, or change data and return it back to the user in the form of front-end code. This person delivers code that runs the platform for a product; sometimes, that comes in the form of a content management system.

- **QA tester:** This person is responsible for testing live pages against design and copy needs to ensure that the product is functional and bug-free. This person will most likely deliver bugs or questions to various team members via a report or tickets in a bug tracking system.

- **Project manager:** Hey, I know this person. He or she will be responsible for planning and facilitating a project. This person will deliver communication plans, project plans, status updates, and more.

- **Account manager:** This role typically only exists on agency teams, and it is responsible for overall client satisfaction and strategy. This person delivers meeting notes and updates on client conversations and decisions.

Depending on where you work and the type of projects you work on, this might seem like a big team. The thing is, not every team uses or needs all of these roles. While there are plenty of specialists out there, there are also plenty of generalists who can do it all. The most important thing to remember is that knowing your team's strengths and weaknesses will help you formulate a plan and create an estimate for completing your project.

Understand the Process and What Works

Once you've got a good grasp on who does what and how, you need to figure out how all of your project's moving parts fit together—or *could* fit together.

You may work for a company that abides by a singular process like Agile, Waterfall, a hybrid of the two, or maybe one of those newfangled processes that's popped up on the internet. Or, hey, maybe you created one all of your own. No matter what process you're using, you should study it, know and understand all of your unknowns, and run with your estimates.

If you work in a place that's more liberal with the process and likes to experiment, make it your mission to understand how things are done and what might happen if you shift things around. For instance, if you work for a construction company, will there be a huge impact if you plan for your baseboards to be painted before the carpet is installed? Sure, you can do it, but will it affect the quality of the work or the time needed to get the work done? (I've done my share of home improvement projects and can comfortably say the answer is "yes." When the carpet installers scratch up those newly painted baseboards, your client will not be happy to learn they will need to be repainted.)

Do everything you can to understand your process, but don't just read a book or a manual. Use the rigid methodology taught in a book or a manual to start conversations about how your team employs a method. Talk to your team, ask questions about what you don't know, and feel free to question how, why, and when things are done. The more you know, the better you can strategize with your team or your clients to find alternate ways to make projects work and save on effort.

Also, always be sure to include your team in any discussions related to estimating projects and process. When estimating projects, talk about the process you might envision taking on with the impending project. This will certainly impact how you think about effort and scope. You'd never want to sign on for a project that the team is not invested in.

Study History

Without a doubt, historical data can help you with new projects; when history is documented, you can analyze the information to create better estimates. A great place to start is asking your team to track their time on tasks, which will give you a better sense for a project's overall level of effort. It's not about cracking the whip or playing big brother and hanging over someone's shoulder—it's being honest about the effort needed to complete a single task.

It goes without saying that every project is unique. Typically, you'll encounter variety in your clients, their communication styles, personalities, constraints, technologies, and so on, but seeing how long your team spent on a certain task or deliverable will give you a sense for estimating a similar task on a new project. The more you work with an individual team member, the better you can estimate what they do, because not only will you know how long it took them to do X, but you'll also know how far off they were on the last estimates they gave you. And the more times you manage a specific task, the better able you will be to judge how long it will take the next time. Over time, you'll have a way to map the experience level of the people doing the work to the amount of time it will take to complete it.

You also might find it very useful to look up old project plans to get a sense for how similar projects were scheduled and how long they took. Just having a general sense of time and deliverables will certainly help when estimating something new.

It's very easy, as a team, to get excited about work and underestimate the time you need to do it. The problem is, when you create inaccurate estimates, you're likely doing everyone a disservice and stressing out over not hitting estimated budgets and timelines. Listen up! Drop the stress. Check your tracked time and plans and use them to help create realistic estimates. If nothing else, reviewing the history to make sure that you're not habitually underestimating is a great practice.

> **NOTE** DON'T WASTE TIME
>
> If you're sensing a potential issue with an estimate, or if expectations are not aligning with an estimate on a possible project, speak up now. There's nothing worse than wasting time estimating a project that might not ever happen anyway.

Get the Pertinent Details

Whether you're estimating a project based on a request for proposal (RFP), a discussion, or an email from a client, you need to know every possible detail of the project before you can provide a realistic estimate. This often means that you have to ask more questions. You never know what kind of errors—or confusion—could be wrapped up in your request for a new project. Don't be bashful! Many stakeholders or product owners don't realize that you need a tremendous amount of information in order to prepare a true and fair estimate. They also might not realize that they already have the answers to your questions.

One of the biggest culprits behind underestimated projects is the lack of pertinent information and background provided on would-be projects. Get your project stakeholders to clear up that gray area and help you break the project down into pieces. That way, you'll be able to create an estimate based on what they need, not what you think they need.

What You Need to Know

It's often easy to take a project request at face value. The problem with doing that is the fact that there are likely a lot of details to uncover. So put your thinking hat on and scrutinize the request. Here are some things to think about on any project request:

- What is the goal of the project? Is it realistic?

- How will you and your client determine if the project is successful?

- What returns will you and your clients see as a result of the project?

- Who will participate from the client side?

- What range of services does the project require?

- What is your client's budget for the project?

- Is there technology involved? If yes, what is the technology?

- Does your client employ anyone with expertise on the topic?

- What is the timeline for the project and will your client require your services after your work is complete?

- Are there any risks associated with the project?

- What would make the project a failure?

- Are there any additional assumptions or dependencies to be aware of?

This list could go on and on depending on the level of information you're provided. Be persistent and get the answers you need. If you're doing this as a precursor to a client project, and your client contact is not inclined to answer every question, take it as a sign. If it's too much to answer a set of questions to help you form a good estimate now, will it be too much for them to be a good partner when the project is underway? Use your judgment in this respect. Not every estimate becomes a real project, so not every request needs to become a real estimate.

> **NOTE** ASK, ASK, ASK
>
> Never be afraid to ask questions about projects to get to the right estimate. Doing so doesn't show weakness in your domain expertise; rather, it shows that you know what to expect, and that you're willing to ask the hard questions to make sure you get it right the first time.

Estimate Time and Materials vs. Fixed-Fee Projects

Before you create an estimate, you'll want to figure out how you should structure your work agreement with your client. In essence, do you want to bill them directly for the time and expenses spent on the project, or do you want to come up with one price to cover everything? It's not an easy thing to figure out, and there are advantages and disadvantages for each. Let's explore it a bit further.

Time and Materials

When you set up a project this way, you'll provide an approximate time estimate to complete the project, but you will bill your client based on an hourly rate and total time spent. So there is an opportunity to make changes on the fly and change the scope as needed. Issues arise when more hours are spent. Remember that clients have an inherent desire to do more and spend less. This fact can mean that a client will be less inclined to explore ideas, make riskier decisions, or possibly even pay for project management services. But that's OK. If you are setting up this type of project, you can set expectations early about how your team operates, how you will manage the work, and how you will communicate about time spent. Doing this will make your clients more comfortable.

Fixed Fee

Creating an estimate for a fixed-fee project means that you are setting parameters around what is in scope for your project, what activities will be performed, and what will be delivered in a specified time frame. There is very little flexibility to change requirements or change approaches in a fixed-fee project, because you're operating on a fixed budget that was based on an estimate of what the project might be. Sounds like a lot of guessing, right? Right.

The following sections explore approaches for making both of these approaches work. Regardless of what you do, establishing some core estimating practices will help you to create more on-target estimates for new projects.

Apply a Work Breakdown Structure

If you're working on a large project and you want to get a sense of how long tasks will take to accomplish, take a step back and figure out how you can attack the project one step at a time. Try to use a work breakdown structure (WBS), which is a well-known traditional project management tactic.

A fixture in classic project management methodology and systems engineering, the WBS is a deliverable-oriented decomposition of a project into smaller components. A work breakdown structure is composed of a hierarchy of specific elements; for example, an element may be a product, data, service, or any combination thereof. A WBS also provides the necessary framework for detailed cost estimating, and it provides guidance for schedule development and control.

Essentially, by using a WBS, you should be able to take a top-down look at your project and break it into the tasks and subtasks that will get you to completion (see Figure 3.1). By breaking your project down into tasks, you'll find that you can start to see the forest through the trees. It's a simple, yet methodical way of organizing and understanding your project scope in smaller, manageable components. Sound easy? Well, maybe not. But keep reading and you'll get there fast.

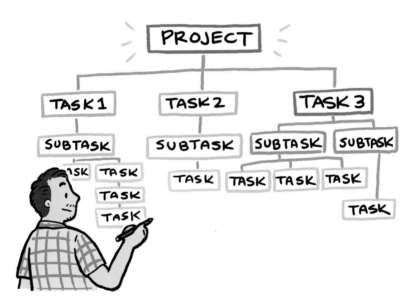

FIGURE 3.1

Creating a WBS can help you break down a project into phases, deliverables, and tasks and then apply effort estimates to them.

How to Use a Work Breakdown Structure

When you're comfortable with the overall process of creating a WBS, you will be able to adapt the practice to any project—from moving your house to building a complex database with 75 offshore teams. That's right, the WBS will be your friend. But before you go off and start creating these documents (and on-point estimates), let's walk through a process that will help ensure a solid, workable estimate.

Step 1: List High-Level Deliverables

If you've got a project scope, you're going to find getting started on your WBS very easy. If you don't have a scope, you better turn right around and talk to your clients or boss about the scope. Starting any project without a scope is dangerous because it sets the stage for what will be delivered and when.

First, sit down with your team and list out what will need to be delivered in order to meet your project's end goal. For instance, if you are building a new website, you might deliver the following items:

- Site map
- Wireframes
- Page designs
- Front-end code
- Back-end code

Make sure that you're being very inclusive of all tasks, and that you're not leaving anything out. For instance, if you're working on a website redesign project, have you accounted for content? If you miss a deliverable now, you will regret it. So, listing things as a team is very helpful, as it ensures that all of your bases are covered. A team conversation will set expectations for who will be responsible for deliverables and tasks, all while engaging the team on the overall process of the project.

Step 2: Think About Tasks

After you've identified the high-level deliverables for your project, you're going to take a deeper look into what actually needs to be done within each one of them individually. This isn't just a simple exercise where you say, "Who will do this and how long will it take?" It goes much deeper than that—and that's a good thing because that is how you will be able to create a better estimate.

As you dig into the high-level deliverables, you should discuss
(or ask yourself):

- What needs to be done to create this deliverable?

- What other related project tasks will contribute to completing
this deliverable successfully?

- What are the requirements of the tasks?

- Are the tasks dependent on other tasks? What should come first?

- Are we cutting any corners here? (Make sure that you list everything and anything—don't cheat yourself!)

As you conduct this exercise, keep in mind that you truly want to
list every possible task that could go into the high-level deliverable.
Remember, the point here is to account for all time so that you can
create a reasonable estimate. You won't be able to do that if you're not
thinking it through properly.

Using the website redesign as an example, here is how you might
break up the first deliverable, which was "Site map":

- Review the current site.

- Test the current structure with five site users.

- Review the test findings.

- Organize the site map in a spreadsheet.

- Review the first low-fidelity version with the team.

- Revise the structure using the team's input.

- Create a visual version of the site map.

- Annotate the sections.

- Write a description of the new site map.

- Present the site map to the clients.

- Review the client feedback.

- Implement the feedback.

- Deliver v2.

- Conduct a meeting with the clients.

- Finalize the site map.

This list of tasks is an estimate for all of the work that will need to be done in order to get to a finalized site map. When you sit down with your team to discuss these tasks, you'll want to be sure that you're operating with a common understanding of how things are done, or that you're at least talking through the process. Listing every single detail will help you spell out the effort it will take to complete the deliverable.

Step 3: Get Granular

Get granular, because you want to make your WBS as detailed as possible. The only way to do that is to examine every step that you've identified and list tasks. It's all about examining effort and determining the work that will need to be done in order to complete the deliverable successfully. If you make an investment to do this, you'll find less room for missed expectations and budget overages in the long term. Using the website redesign as an example, here is how you might break up the deliverable, which was "Test the current structure with five site users":

- Recruit users.
- Schedule sessions.
- Write the test script.
- Conduct five sessions.
- Compensate users for their time.
- Write up the findings and recommendations.

This one task is proof that any single line item in a scope can be an expensive one! Not only did this example include six subtasks, but also a line item that required payment to an outside party. You'll want to know about these expenses in advance of scoping your project, and your clients will, too. So be sure to account for them early on so that nothing comes as a surprise.

Step 4: Format and Estimate

Traditionally, you'll find that work breakdown structures are presented in flow charts that resemble website site maps. That format works well because it shows a hierarchy of tasks and is easily numbered and referred back to. But some people like to list them on whiteboards or put them in spreadsheets. The format isn't what matters here—it's the completeness and accuracy of the tasks included.

When you've listed all of your tasks and subtasks in a format that makes sense, you'll want to re-review it and make sure that you've included everything. Once that's confirmed, go through the list and discuss each task in terms of the level of effort. This could be in minutes, hours, days, or weeks—it really depends on how granular you need to get and how your organization estimates projects. Assigning an increment of time to each task will help you add up a total estimate of time (and possible costs) and create a project plan when you get to that step in your project. When you're done, you will know if you're in scope, out of scope, or actually operating on another planet. It's true that you might run this exercise and find that you've articulated too much time or effort to do everything within the scope of the project. The good thing is that you've set the baseline for what's needed, and you can scale back on tasks to fit the scope or the timeline.

Here is a very basic WBS for a very common deliverable—moving (see Figure 3.2). Check out the tasks and every aspect related to the event that the author has taken into consideration. Is anything missing?

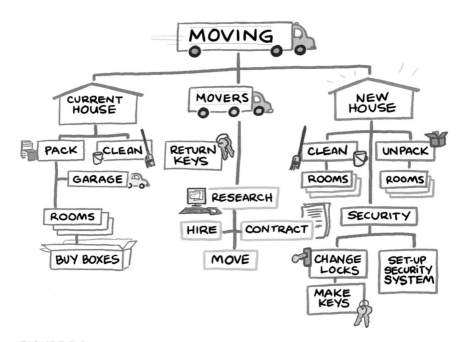

FIGURE 3.2

Here's an example of a WBS I created before I moved. Full disclosure: my estimates were off!

If you estimate your projects based on units—whether it is weeks, days, or hours—using a WBS will help you understand very quickly if your estimate will exceed the intended budget. Let's take this example further and assign estimated hours to each step, but just remember that it could change when you dig into the actual work. (These time estimates should be based on a combination of experience and hypotheses.)

Current House	
Kitchen	1 day
Bathroom	half day
Bedroom 1	half day
Bedroom 2	half day
Living Room	1 day
Dining Room	1 day
Basement	2 days
Garage	2 days
Total	**8.5 days***

* Sum of tasks includes wrapping objects, packing in boxes, and prepping for movers.

This type of exercise can be extremely helpful during the sales process when a client tells you they have X dollars to spend. Based on your estimates, you can easily map a set of tasks or deliverables to something that works for both the dollar amount and the client's goals. And, if a potential client comes back and says, "Well that seems a little more than we want to spend," you can lean on your work breakdown structure to negotiate the cost down based on what's included in your scope. For instance, if I had to cut down on the cost/time of moving based on the hours that I estimated, I could likely remove the "cleaning" step from my "moving" WBS (though I'm sure someone might be unhappy about that). Use the WBS to your advantage this way, and you'll not only create a project estimate that maps to a specific budget, but you'll also work out a solid set of project requirements.

Estimating Agile-ish Projects

Before diving into the brave world of Agile, it's important to note here that your project stakeholders need to be OK with having a fixed time frame and budget but a variable scope if you're going to take a more agile approach. This works really well when you're on an in-house team, but can be particularly difficult if you're working at an agency or just with clients. It's typical to vary the scope with Agile in order to achieve a result that's defined at a high level. In fact, you could make the time or budget variable as well, but that has its trade-offs. It's not advisable to make everything variable, though. That's usually a mess.

NOTE SCRUM? WHAT THE?

"Scrum" is a silly word with a big meaning. It's an Agile software development model based on a self-organizing, dedicated team working on one project, iteratively to completion. The term is named for the scrum (or scrummage) formation in rugby, which is used to restart the game after an event that causes play to stop, such as an infringement.

Many teams have moved to an Agile process (mostly Scrum), or at least are picking up parts of it in an effort to be more nimble and efficient. It's very exciting! Making Scrum effective when you're working with a client or internal stakeholder can be a challenge. Some teams embrace Agile by running entire projects in sprints, or set periods of time during which specific work has to be completed and made ready for review. This works quite well when stakeholders embrace their roles, can make decisions quickly, and actively take part in team discussions.

Other teams take a more hybrid approach and apply the same idea of sprints, but after research and design is complete. This tends to work better when working with external stakeholders or clients who can't make decisions alone—or quickly—and need to be guided through a project rather than actively play a role in it. Whether you're using Agile with a capital "A" or trying to be more agile to deliver your projects more quickly, you will want to remember some very core values that make Agile work.

Dedicated Teams

If you're truly working Agile, you'll require a full-time team working on a project. This can be difficult in an agency setting, but it makes estimating easier. Here are some things to consider when assembling teams:

- What roles do you need?

- How much time is considered "full-time"?

- How will you think about company meetings, management tasks, etc.?

- Will your team be truly dedicated? (Are there any other projects happening, pulling their time away?)

- Will there be holidays or time off during the project?

- Is there a blended rate for the team?

You should also make sure that your clients understand the ideas behind your version of Agile and how you can make it work with them. More importantly, you will want them to understand how they will need to be involved in the process. In fact, you might want to define your client's role and explain to them what it means to the process. There's more on that at the end of this section.

Sprints

In the Scrum method, work is confined to a regular, repeatable work cycle, known as a *sprint*. The timing of the sprint is typically determined by the team, but you'll see sprints that range from one week to one month. Regardless of the timebox you choose, know that working in sprints requires the focus of a dedicated team. During each sprint, it's up to the team to create a shippable product or feature. Because projects require multiple sprints, each iteration of work builds on the previous one, building on or even replacing some of the previous work. You see, Scrum is loose, but the sprints provide the structure needed to keep the project on track.

Every sprint begins with the sprint planning meeting, where the team and product owner determine what work will be conducted over the course of the sprint. Then, after work is in progress during the sprint, team members check in with each other daily at a stand-up meeting. Finally, after the sprint is complete, the entire team conducts a sprint review and a retrospective meeting to review and demo the work done and discuss how things have gone.

A lot of planning and effort goes into a sprint, not only to execute the work, but also to make sure that you've given yourself the right amount of time to get it done. But how do all of these sprints add up to a deadline? Well, Scrum is iterative, which means you can launch and iterate. But we all know some projects have hard deadlines. Knowing your project's deadline will help you determine how many sprints you need. And knowing the team dedicated to the project will help estimate the cost.

Scrum Team Meetings

A lot of time goes into making sure that Scrum teams are communicating and are on task. In effect, this ensures that projects are delivered on strategy and on time! Below is a list of meetings that typically take place on Scrum teams:

- **Sprint planning:** A team planning meeting that determines what to complete in the coming sprint.

- **Daily stand-up:** Also known as a *daily scrum*, a 15-minute mini-meeting for the software team to sync.

- **Sprint demo:** A sharing meeting where the team shows what they've shipped in that sprint.

- **Sprint retrospective:** A review of what did and didn't go well with actions to make the next sprint better.

So What Does It Mean for Your Client?

Clients working with agency Scrum teams cannot sit back and wait for deliverables to come to them to review. They are an active member of the team and have daily insight into the operations of the project, and in some sense, they control it. So that means that they have to account for a fair amount of time spent with the team, and they have to consider how they make decisions and communicate with their own teams. When you're running sprints, you are able to iterate, but feedback has to be timely and decisions have to be made quickly.

It also means that clients can always depend on a fixed sprint cost for any additional change or request. When they ask for a new feature, you can say, "OK, it will take one more sprint to complete that," and they will immediately know the cost. Pretty great, right?

Using the two principles described previously, the outline that follows illustrates how you can create an estimate for a modified Scrum process. For the purposes of this example, imagine that a client is asking for a website redesign project to be completed in six months. This example implies a sample rate, using a monthly blended rate of $2,500 for the individual. You can easily come up with this monthly number by multiplying the number of estimated billable hours for an individual per week by the rate. That means there will be some work for you to do in order to start, but it's fairly simple if you've got the information you need on hand.

1 RESOURCE, 4 WEEKS = $10,000

This means that the cost for one person to work on a project for 4 weeks is $10,000.

2-WEEK SPRINTS

Most projects operate on 2-week sprints to get sizeable chunks of work done to review as a team and with your client.

1 RESOURCE, 1 SPRINT = $5,000

Given the monthly rate, this is what it will cost for 1 team member to work on your project per sprint.

6 MONTHS = 12 SPRINTS

If your project is 6 months long, you might work 12 sprints. It's important to check calendars to see if you have to adjust sprints or timing due to the calendar. If you don't do this, you will end up with an inaccurate estimate.

4 RESOURCES, 12 SPRINTS

Let's say you only need 4 people on this project over 12 weeks.

4 x $5,000 = $20,000 x 12

Simple math here—the number of people multiplied by the individual cost per sprint gives you a total cost per sprint. Multiplying that by the number of sprints will give you the total cost of the project: $240,000

Of course, this is never going to be perfect. And it requires dedication to the process. But, wow, does it make estimating easy! You'll always need to watch out for the usual project suspects: additional requirements, late or missing client feedback, missed meetings, and so on. But do your best to define roles and meetings early on.

For instance, if you are using the Agile team roles on your project, define who fills them. Most likely, you will want to use this kind of setup:

- Scrum Team
- Product Owner: Client
- Scrum Master: Agency PM
- Development Team: Agency Creative and Technical Team

What does this mean? Well, it means that your client is an active member of the team who helps set the course of each sprint and makes decisions on the areas of focus on your project. The client is truly leading your team while your team's PM is facilitating. That requires a lot of time!

Estimate Tasks for Agile Projects

Once you're embedded on a team and are running an Agile methodology, you'll quickly find that you're up against estimating tasks rather than the big picture project. In effect, by running sprints, you're taking sips from a water fountain rather than drinking from the fire hose.

An advantage of working in the Agile methodology is that you involve everyone on your team to create realistic estimates. Because each team member brings a different perspective to the table, and they can clearly articulate the work that is required of them on a single task, you'll find that creating estimates can be easy as a team. This open way of discussing what's needed can uncover potential issues, changes to workflow, and sometimes the need for outside expertise. Go ahead and round your team up for an hour and estimate tasks together.

User Stories

If you're not familiar with the Agile methodology, you might confuse the term "user story" with a self-written tome on the day in a life of a person who uses your product. Well, kind of, but not really! A user story is a tool used in the Agile methodology to capture a description of a project feature from an end-user's perspective. The user story describes the type of user, what they want, and why. A user story helps create a simplified description of a requirement, and can lead you to a very distinct estimate for the design and build of that requirement.

> **NOTE** A TYPICAL USER STORY STATEMENT
>
> An example user story statement might be **As a** (ROLE) **I want to** (DESIRED ACTION) **so I can** (WHY I WANT TO DO THIS).

Forget Weeks, Days, and Hours . . . Use Story Points

The most basic way to estimate a task is in what we know as hours, days, weeks, or months. The Agile methodology erases your memory of any estimates created with increments of time and requires a different way of thinking about estimates: story points. This is a number that tells the team how difficult the user story (or feature) is, due to complexity, unknowns, and effort. Teams use different scales to determine story points. Some might use the following: extra small,

small, medium, large, and extra large. More commonly, Agile teams use variations of the Fibonacci sequence to estimate effort:

0, 0.5, 1, 2, 3, 5, 8, 13, 20, 40, 100.

The most confusing part of using story points is determining what the numbers actually mean in relation to effort. For instance, how do you know that a "3" means the same thing to the whole team? The best way to determine this with a first-time team is to sit down and define the story points together. Take one story, dissect it together, and determine that you're all in agreement on the ratings. This might mean that you change or simplify the sequence or come up with your own rating system. That is completely fine—what matters most is that you're working with the same understanding of the scoring.

Planning Poker

Want to have some fun with estimation? Planning poker is a game that team members can play during planning meetings to come up with collaborative estimates using story points (see sidebar). This game requires the full project team in order to ensure that everyone on the team understands the stories and has a chance to voice concerns and provide input into estimation.

The coolest part about story points is that they require you to keep estimates on the lower side. If a story is rated at the upper limit, the team should reassess it and possibly even break it up into smaller

Make Your Own Planning Poker Cards

You can have some fun by designing and making your own decks as a team, or check out these nicely designed cards by Redbooth. They're available for free on Github under a creative commons license: https://github.com/redbooth/Scrum-poker-cards

To begin, each team member is given a set of cards with your team's selected rating system on them. One person reads the user story, and each team member holds up a card that represents the level of effort for that story. Scores may vary, and that is normal, but in order to get to an agreement, ask the team members with the lowest and highest estimates to explain their scores. Through discussion, the team will come up with a final score and document it with their stories.

stories. The goal here isn't to get deep into the nitty-gritty details of every task like you would with a WBS. It's to keep it at a high level so that you have a high-level understanding of the level of effort, so you can then flow it into your sprint with complementary tasks.

> **NOTE** HAVE SOME FUN
>
> Collaborative meetings should be fun and foster a sense of team unity. If there's debate, keep it light and seek to resolve it quickly. If scoring takes too long, you may be overthinking it. Drop it for the time being and come back to it.

Why Stories and Points?

Still not sold on story points? Here are a few reasons why Agile experts prefer to use points (it's all very psychological!):

- **Dates can never account for the unexpected work and life elements that come up on a daily basis.** Using story points pulls all of that cruft out of day-to-day operations and allows you to focus just on the task. Never mind meetings, Slack conversations, impromptu discussions, and all of the other things that pull you away from your tasks; points will score just the work.

- **Holidays, birthdays, anniversaries—they all imply an emotional connection.** And they are dates. Story points focus on just the complexity of the task, no matter when it is being completed (so forget about missing a task, or work, for your gran's birthday).

- **We all work differently.** You might be able to accomplish a task in less time than your teammate, but that doesn't matter. Each person is assigned a story and can rate it based on how they will approach it—and that is completely acceptable. This methodology allows the team to work at its own pace and meet commitments on their estimates.

- **You can't track time while running Agile projects.** It defeats the purpose of points and can confuse your team when estimating.

> **NOTE** YOU CAN ADAPT PRACTICES
>
> You can always do your own thing. Be a consummate learner and understand different estimating techniques. This will help you to come up with processes of your own.

Get Your Estimates In

Are you ready to dig in and estimate a project of your own? Whether you're going to break projects down to tasks and hours or use the Agile story points system, you'll want to give it a test run and try it out for size. Make up a project of your own and list all of the steps or user stories that need to go into completing a project. (It can be something simple like moving.) Run it by someone else and see what that person thinks. Did you miss anything? Did you underestimate the hours? Are the stories on-point? Doing a test run will get you ready for your first real estimate, or hone your skills for your next one.

You'll find that there is no right or wrong way to create an estimate; it's consistency that matters. Your own personal style of estimating projects will include a mixture of project knowledge, historical review, client inquisition, and a ton of gut instinct.

TL; DR

New projects pop up often. Before you dive in, you need to know some basic information about how long the new project might take, or how much it will cost. When time is tight, all you need to do is:

- Understand the project.

- Know who on your team can do what and when.

- Look back at similar projects to see how they were done and how long they took (or what they cost).

- Ask questions to fill the gaps on what you don't know related to the new project.

- Create a new estimate:

  - List tasks and apply time estimates.

  - Create user stories and apply a rating system to them to understand their complexity.

- GET TO WORK!

Getting to Know Your Projects

Gain the confidence to get the information you need out of people, even in the most stressful situations. You'll be proud of yourself for it.

I have a storied past when it comes to jobs. I've worked at start-ups, in higher education, at agencies, and as a consultant. I'm happy to have landed this most recent job as my own boss, because I didn't have to go through the interviewing process. I like to think I'm a good interviewee, but I recognize that what I expect of the interview experience may not be in line with the interviewer... or interviewers.

In the early 2000s, I was on a search for a new job because the dot-com I was working for was on the verge of explosion. I went for an interview with a well-known retailer in New York City to be their producer. I was excited about the opportunity and did my research before getting into the interview. I found out everything I could about the new role, the company, its employees, and most importantly, the people who would be in my interview. I showed up confident in my suit and tie.

The interviews went really well. It felt like the right fit. The people were great—we were having a conversation. It never felt like an interview. As I thought the conversation was coming to a close, they asked if I could hang around for another hour to meet more people. I couldn't decline. I wanted it. Within five minutes, three executives came into the room and grilled me for about 45 minutes. It was intense, uncomfortable, and completely different from my previous interactions. I immediately felt like it was over, but I was not about to give up.

I turned the tables on them when they asked me if I had any questions. I immediately asked them to tell me about their backgrounds, their tenure with the company, and how they might see this new producer helping them achieve their goals. Honestly, I was amazed by my courage and ability to think so quickly, but I wanted it, and I knew that I had to win them over. The only way to do that was to get to know them, because success always comes out of making connections and understanding other people's motivations.

In the end, the interview turned around. I was able to command a presence and enjoy the second part of the interview as much as the first. But it took some work! That doesn't mean I left feeling great. In fact, I left confused. I wanted the job, but something just did not feel right about the experience I had. And when the offer for the job came in, I was able to assess the situation in a critical way. Did I want to work for an organization that tried to blindside its employees and intimidate them? No. So when I declined the offer, I told them why.

I let them know that it felt like a red flag to me—not one that I was willing to take on. Instead, I eventually lost my job and moved back home with my parents to find a much less glamorous job in higher education. The rest is history.

• • •

There is no doubt that having a full understanding of your project—and the people involved—will help you manage it better. There are so many important details to be uncovered through just a bit of investigation. The thing is, you have to make time for it. As soon as you've agreed on a project scope—or maybe even before there's a contract in place—someone (typically a stakeholder or client) will inevitably ask you for a project plan. Be careful about planning without knowing the full details of the project. While a plan is fairly easy to construct, remind everyone involved that the journey of creating a plan does not consist of sitting down and writing up your approach and dumping it into your project planning tool of choice. In fact, that's the opposite of how you should handle it.

A solid plan is created after you've done your own project management research about the team, your clients, and your project and have determined all of the factors that will make that plan change. You should build a plan with inevitable changes or delays in mind. Make sure that you've done your due diligence by asking about the factors that could delay your project, but go beyond that: good project managers plan for the unplanned. They do this by devising an optimal route through the project, with contingencies and backups in place and ready to go. If you have a solid construct for why you built a plan a certain way, you'll be able to roll with the changes and quickly communicate time delays and impacts.

Start with Research

Before you start a plan, you have to stop yourself and make sure that you know all of the facts. Take a deep breath and then dive into the documents and communications relevant to the project. Print the scope of work and all the details that come along with it (maybe an RFP or notes from sales calls or meetings with your client team) and read them end to end. Be thorough. Understand the details and ask thoughtful questions before you commit to anything. A good project manager is well-informed and methodical in the way he or she guides a project. At a minimum, you'll be responsible for possessing a thorough understanding of the following information:

- What are the goals of the project?

- Do you know your client's needs and expectations?

- What is the makeup of your client team and their decision-making process (i.e., how they'll review and approve your team's work), which might answer these questions:

  - Who is the project sponsor and how available is that person?

  - What does success on this project mean to them personally?

  - Who is the client-side PM and will they plan on being in constant contact with you (they need to be)?

  - Who are the additional stakeholders your team should be aware of? What does success on this project look like to each of them?

In addition to all of your questions about your client team and their expectations, set some time aside with your main client contact and ask them some tough questions about process, organizational politics, general risks, and what project failure looks like (and means) to them. Doing so will not only convey that your team has the experience to handle any type of difficult personalities or situation, but it also shows that you care about the project and want it to run smoothly.

Getting the Most Out of Stakeholder Interviews

If you're running a full-scale project, chances are your team is going to conduct stakeholder interviews. These interviews with a variety of people and positions can give your team a very clear understanding of goals, challenges, feature requests, and even personalities within the organization. Be sure to use this time to ask important questions about the success of the project and how you might navigate the organization to ensure that your project is discussed, understood, and becomes a complete success.

If you are not conducting the interviews yourself, suggest some of the questions from the previous list to incorporate into conversations with higher-level stakeholders. It's best to get a deeper understanding of the culture around projects and how they are run, so talk about it with a

- Has your team discussed how you will gather feedback?

- Who is the final sign-off? Or who owns the project?

- What is the project deadline? What are the factors or events that are calling for that date (a meeting, an ad campaign, an event)? What is the business impact of not meeting that date?

- Are there any dates when you will be closed or not available?

- Will there be any meetings or points in the project where you'll want to present on the current project status to a larger group (i.e., a board meeting)?

- Has your team been through a project like this in the past?

- How did it go?

- Is there anything that would prevent the project from being successful?

- Is there a preferred mode of communication? Are there any communication plans in place that you should know about? Will those modes or plans differ by person or department?

- Are there any points in the process that some stakeholders might not understand that you can explain?

- Is there a stakeholder you need to consider who is not on your list (a president, dean, the boss's wife)?

variety of people to get a true, well-rounded perspective. Questions about how projects have worked in the past and how decisions are made, combined with questions about goals and values can truly help inform your approach to managing the project and its stakeholders.

At the same time, be sure to record these interviews. If you're able to sit in on the call, great! Take copious notes and listen for details that will help your team understand the organization and how your project may roll out. Listen for comments about the following:

- Ownership of processes, documents, and tools

- Politics surrounding decisions

- Opinions about similar projects, design, process, communications, etc.

- Related projects, partners, and possible dependencies
- Details about routine meetings, presentations, holidays, outages, etc.
- Details around the launch of your project (events, campaigns, meetings, etc.)
- Mention of other stakeholders, relationships, disagreements, etc.

Just listen and take notes. Anything that could be a project risk or potential issue to think about is something you should call out and eventually discuss with your team and your main point of contact. If one nugget of truth about an opinion, person, issue, or process is raised and you can adjust your plan slightly to avoid a major problem, you win! And we all like winning.

Depending on the size of the organization you're working with, you might have to do some fact-finding to figure out who those players are so that you can understand what makes them tick. It's your job to make sure that you're playing the politics of the organization you're working in or with. It sounds somewhat daunting, but you can take some very simple steps to identify and understand the people who can make or break your projects.

> **NOTE** ASK FOR HELP
>
> There is no way that you can be all-knowing when it comes to the ins and outs of an org chart and all of the politics that might come with it. Make that known and ask for the help you need when it comes to identifying and understanding stakeholders. Or do some Google or LinkedIn magic (read: stalking) of your own to get information about stakeholder roles, histories, and organizational roles and interests.

Identify the Players

If you're working with a client organization, chances are that you have no idea who the top brass are and how to get in touch with them. But you want to make sure that you're accounting for them in your process. Are they concerned about your digital project? If they aren't, are they comfortable with someone else calling the shots? Get answers to these questions by working with your client or project sponsor to help you determine how the decision-making process will impact your project. Whether you're working with a client or an internal team, mapping out their hierarchy and involvement level will help you make decisions on what you deliver and how those deliverables will be circulated through the organization.

The size of the client organization and the number of approval layers will affect any plan. Of course, not all organizations will be the same size, but the roles in the organization tend to stay similar. You might work with a very small team, but consider asking about the hierarchy in the organization based on the number of iterations you expect on deliverables. Here are some very high-level groupings to think about across any organization.

Avoid the "Swoop and Poop"

Before you do anything, be sure that you know and understand what motivates the people who will make the decisions on your project (see Figure 4.1). After all, if you leave them out, you might end up at square one after doing a whole lot of work. That's right, they could swoop in like a big ol' bird and poop all over the work you did, just because they can! So you need to do everything you can to avoid it.

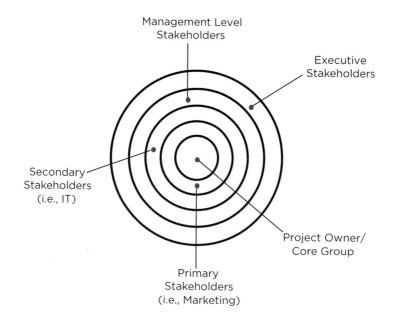

FIGURE 4.1

Be sure to think through all of the layers of stakeholders who may exist. Sit down with your clients to review who may be involved in your project at critical points.

- **Project Owner/Core Group:** These are the people who are responsible for the day-to-day success of the project. They came up with the idea (and likely the budget) for the project, they wrote the RFP for the project, found the right team to work with, and will hold most of the answers about the project. Your point of contact sits on this team and is responsible for making sure that things go well on their side of things.

- **Primary Stakeholders:** These are the people who are most connected to the goals of your project. They're invested in what you're doing and took part in sponsoring the project. One of these people—or their supervisor—may sit on this team. On many digital projects, this might be a marketing team.

- **Secondary Stakeholders:** This team may not have written the goals for the project, but they will be a part of making sure it is a success. Or maybe they have some sort of responsibility for the project. On many digital projects, this might be an IT team.

- **Management Level Stakeholders:** These people aren't the doers, but they are the decision makers—possibly the people who oversee the primary and secondary teams, or even the people who oversee a whole division of the organization you're working with. These people tend to be very connected to the vision of the organization and how your project can succeed, so you want to understand their goals, set their expectations for the project, and keep them close.

- **Executive Stakeholders:** These people pay the bills. They make all the important decisions, and they can completely kill your project if they feel out of the loop. So do your due diligence and get to know who they are, and what their motivations are. These people could be C- or executive-level people within organizations. They may also be on a board of trustees, directors, or something similar. This means they're not in the day-to-day operation of the company, but oversee it. You'll want to think through ways to engage them.

NOTE BEWARE THE SNEAKY STAKEHOLDER

Always ask if there's someone you haven't met and should consider. You want to uncover unknown stakeholders who may be hiding behind the boardroom doors just waiting to step in. These people could be deans in colleges, remote board members, executives who travel a lot, the boss's spouse, or anyone else who may not seem obvious to you. Everyone has an opinion, and it's your job to make sure they're heard at the right times.

This Template Is Practical in Use!

I developed this template shown in Figure 4.2 as a whiteboarding exercise when I was working with an organization that claimed to be "flat." That worried me, because I knew there would be some sort of politics when it came to making decisions. Presenting these high-level groups helped my clients understand the layers of people in various departments that would eventually become a part of the project. My intuition was correct, and together we mapped out our stakeholder teams and then came up with a plan for how we'd handle presentations, meetings, project updates, and approvals.

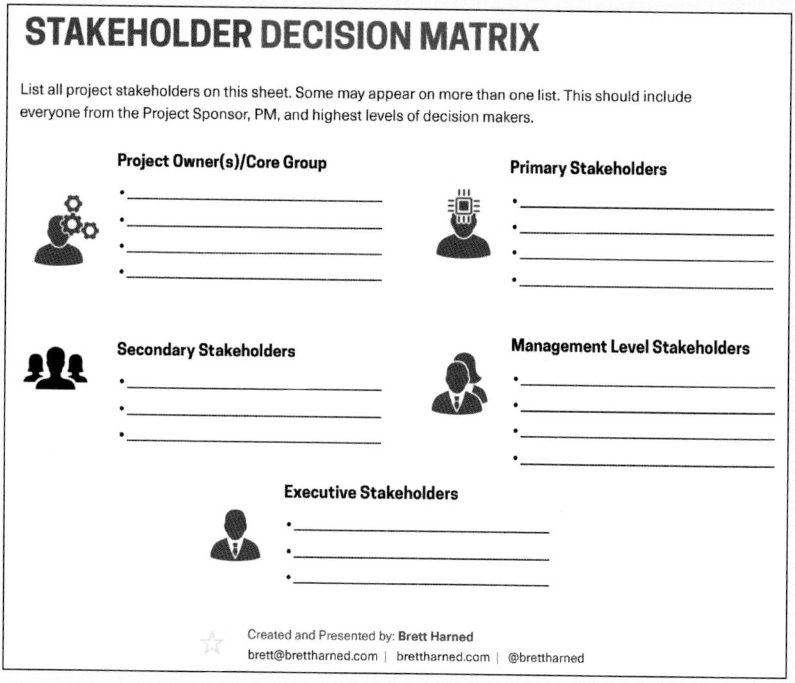
STAKEHOLDER DECISION MATRIX
List all project stakeholders on this sheet. Some may appear on more than one list. This should include everyone from the Project Sponsor, PM, and highest levels of decision makers.
Project Owner(s)/Core Group
Primary Stakeholders
Secondary Stakeholders
Management Level Stakeholders
Executive Stakeholders
Created and Presented by: Brett Harned
brett@bretttharned.com | bretttharned.com | @bretttharned

FIGURE 4.2
Use a version of this stakeholder decision matrix to map out your project's stakeholders and how they will be involved in the process.

Talk About the Work

Let's face it—your project isn't totally about the people. It's about the work. But if you don't fully explain the intent of the work and how it might affect other areas of your project, you're going to confuse and upset someone.

It's very important to think about and discuss the types of deliverables you'll work on and present during your project, and present them in the context of how decisions will be made on the project. If you have not planned your project approach, think through the types of deliverables your team will create. List them by project phase and discuss them with your stakeholders. Be sure to detail the type of documents, designs, templates, etc., you will deliver. Dig in and talk about their intent, their dependencies, and overall importance to the success of the project.

An in-depth conversation about deliverables will lead to conclusions about who will need to be involved with reviews and responses at the deliverable level. Never forget to ask, "Who is the final approval on this deliverable?"

> **NOTE** SHOW SAMPLE WORK
>
> It's a good practice to have some white-labeled work on hand to share with your stakeholders. Showing a simple example of what a deliverable looks like and how it may be presented can help stakeholders understand what level of education will be needed, who will need to be involved, and possibly even how long it may take to review it with a team.

If it's helpful and you want to formalize things (which is recommended on particularly large projects), map out a stakeholder decision matrix, as seen in Figure 4.2. First, sit down with your point of contact to outline the decision-making groups (as listed previously in this chapter) and then map out the deliverables that go along with them. At the same time, be crystal clear about how the decision-making process will impact the progress you make on a project. For instance, what would happen if a stakeholder came in and decided to reverse a decision on an approval of your very first deliverable? If you let your stakeholders know the impact of their disorganization before they even get to that point, you'll avoid potential disasters.

The best way to help stakeholders understand how they can ruin the progress of a project and miss deadlines is to share similar project stories. If you're feeling overly dramatic, show them the first version of your project plan next to the last version. There's nothing more impactful than a real-life example of a disaster to keep you on your game to avoid your own disaster.

Getting to Know Your Clients Can Help!

I managed a website redesign project for a very large organization that had several departments involved in the project. Every department had a stake in the project, and they all thought their piece of the project was the most important. After sitting in on stakeholder interviews and doing my own investigation into the people on the project, I knew I was in for a real challenge when it came to feedback and approvals. In fact, when I asked my clients about who owned the project, they told me that it was *seven* people. **RED FLAG!**

You see, seven people cannot own one project. Maybe they can contribute to it, or be involved in some way, but there's no way that seven people will agree on the same decisions all the time. So it was my job to break the news to them: Having seven decision makers would be a pretty sizeable risk on the project, and our timeline and budget might suffer if they were unable to agree on decisions within our already established timeline. Of course, they told me they would handle it. In that case, all I could do was call out the issue.

Fast-forward three months: our team had delivered design concepts to five of the seven stakeholders, because two of them had missed the very important meeting. Not shockingly, the client was one week late with feedback. I inquired daily about feedback and finally heard that not all feedback was in, and that there was disagreement. My immediate response wasn't "*I told you so!*" (as much as I wanted it to be). Instead, I sat down with my main point of contact and discussed the issues and the impact to the timeline—and eventually the budget. I also recommended that we revisit the decision-making process. If two people were not placing enough importance on the decisions, maybe they should be asked to step down. It wasn't an easy recommendation to actually say, but it had to be done.

In the end, I had to tell my clients that it was my job to call out red flags (or risks) as I saw them. They respected the fact that I was there to keep things in check, but, of course, they did as they pleased. What does that mean? Well, they kept all seven stakeholders, were late with feedback, and disagreed quite often. Here's the thing: I didn't care that they did that, because I was able to clearly state the issues and the impacts every time one came up. In turn, we were able to extend the timeline and the budget when it was necessary.

I really like being brutally honest about project red flags, and clients usually do, too. It can be quite difficult to do, because sometimes it requires calling out where your clients are being difficult or flat-out dysfunctional. That's when it gets tricky, and you have to use a certain level of decorum when communicating details. But, in the end, calling out the risks and knowing about them will help you.

Heed the Red Flag

You are bound to hear some things during the course of a project that will make you cringe. Or giggle. Or just be flat-out angry. An age-old example of this is when a potential new client asks to see your team's creative approach to their project before signing a contract. We call it "spec work" in the design industry, and we really dislike it, because it requires work to be done for free with no promise of winning a project. And the work has to be done in a vacuum without the benefit of research, process, or even a simple conversation with key stakeholders. This is a frustrating scenario that happens all too often on projects.

Red flags and general project issues are unfortunately normal. As a PM, you are never going to be 100 percent happy about everything project-related. But you can do everything in your power *not* to make those cringe-worthy facts full-blown issues. Here are some scenarios that should make you raise the red flag with your team and your stakeholders (as painful as that may be).

- **Stakeholders or team members who have no interest in talking about how the project gets done.** Everyone has to take part in the project process in order to make it a complete success. They don't all have to be in the weeds with you, but they should have a general interest and understanding of how things work. It's your job to keep them informed. If they aren't showing interest, raise that flag and have a conversation with them to understand why they're disinterested and come up with a plan that works for you and them.

- **Stakeholders who don't have clear answers about decision makers.** Someone has to have the final say on your project. If no one knows who that is, or is not taking responsibility, you will have problems actually completing your project. Be sure to have a conversation about the types of decisions and approvals that are required to make the project a success...or just to complete it. This may be a few people on some projects due to hierarchy, subject matter expertise, or even interest in the project. You may even find that design, technology, and content involve different teams of people on your project. Keep that in mind when getting started and push to identify the right people for the process and discuss it with them.

- **Stakeholders who underestimate the time it will take to get approvals.** It's always tough to estimate the time it will take other people to review and comment on things. Project managers know this. Stakeholders? Not as much. If a stakeholder tells you that their team of six will have feedback to you in 24 hours, raise that red flag. It may be an ideal situation that day, but what happens when one of the six is out? Or in meetings? It's your job to help them think through those scenarios and make your plan realistic.

- **Stakeholders who invite everyone to everything.** You know the scenario: You walk into a room to present a design, and it seems like everyone, including the interns, are there to give you feedback. It's tough to ask people to leave a meeting, so do your due diligence before meetings and walk the clients through the decision-making matrix. Or give them a suggested list of attendees before the meeting. Avoid design by committee, however you can, and your team will thank you for it.

- **Stakeholders who are not familiar with your type of project.** OK, this isn't as much of a red flag as it is a warning that you had better put your educator's hat on. You might have to make some extra time to explain why, how, and when you do things on your project. Or maybe spend some time in advance of a presentation to explain the ins and outs to your main point of contact so they can inform your team. Sure, it will take you more time to do, but if you do it well, you will save a lot of time and make yourself and your stakeholders look and feel smart.

- **Team members who work in silos.** We all need our space and time to get work done. But we all know there is no "I" in team, right? Well, sometimes, as the PM you have to remind others that they have to check in with the team on their work. The best thing you can do when someone seems to be disconnecting is to check in with them to see what they are doing. Or even better: require a regular team check-in so that everyone is accountable to report on the work they are doing (or not doing).

- **Stakeholders who want too much in too little time.** Typical. People always want more work done faster. I mean, I wanted this book done last year! Too bad, it's not possible. Again, you have to put your educator's hat on and explain why you have to take certain steps and why they take so long. A simple description, or even a work breakdown structure (see Chapter 3, "Start with an Estimate"), can help to set the pace of your project.

- **Big, awesome, amazing ideas!** There's no doubt that, as a PM, you should encourage collaboration and creativity on your projects. After all, you want the team to be happy with what they produce, and when they are free to create, they will be amazing. But at the same time, you need to watch out for your scope. Keep an eye on what's being discussed, designed, or built and make sure that the whole team is doing the same. If they aren't, there is a chance that you'll collectively lose track of scope and create a red flag together. And you know what happens then: You have to figure out a plan B, or ask the client if they're willing to change the scope of the project. Not fun.

- **Stakeholders with a tendency to gossip.** You're a likeable person. There will be times when stakeholders get comfortable with you and start divulging too much information about what happens behind closed office doors. *Do. Not. Engage.* Always keep it professional and never take sides. Your first responsibility is your project, and you want to make sure it is completed on time and under budget. Don't let any stakeholder disagreements or politics get in your way. If they do, you might just have to engage a senior stakeholder to sort out the madness.

Defining Working Relationships

by Paul Boag
UX designer/consultant, speaker, and author of several books including Digital Adaptation *and* User Experience Revolution

Our client had another project for us. At face value, this sounded great. But the last time we worked with them, it was a nightmare! Our point of contact was a confrontational kind of guy who enjoyed pushing his luck. We had gone through endless iterations, and he had ended up micromanaging design decisions.

After much debate, we decided we would accept the new project. But this time, we were determined that things would be different. For a start, I wanted to define the working relationship.

Of course, I didn't want the project to begin with a confrontation. So in the initial meeting, we talked a little bit about roles. I made no mention of the previous project, instead suggesting that it might be nice to have a clearer definition of who was doing what.

I proposed that the client should champion the users' needs and business objectives. After all, I argued, he understood both of them better than we did. That massaged his ego! My hope was this would move him away from personal opinion toward more objective decision-making.

I also encouraged him to focus on identifying problems with the user experience design and its job in fulfilling business needs. In turn, it was our responsibility to find solutions. I explained that by sharing problems and not solutions, he would get more from the designer. It would push him to come up with better solutions and give the client more value for his money.

I was encouraged that this seemed to go down well. The client enjoyed having something specific to focus on. He also relished the idea of challenging our designer with problems. I confess I was a little nervous as to what would happen as a result.

All went well to begin with. But the point came when he fell back into bad habits. He started asking us to make color changes and tweak the layout. As the designer ramped up for confrontation, I decided to give the client a quick call. I gently pointed out that he had started to focus on solutions rather than problems. I reminded him that we needed to understand the underlying issue. Only then could we challenge the designer to come up with something even better.

I was over the moon when he turned around and apologized for forgetting what he had agreed upon! He then took the time to explain the problem as he saw it. As it turned out, his solution made a lot of sense once we understood the underlying issue. Even the designer grudgingly agreed.

This was not the last time that the client fell into the habit of suggesting solutions rather than problems. But now that I had established clear responsibilities and processes, it was easier to nudge the client back on track. Sometimes the suggestions the client makes are good ones. But often, the designer comes up with something better. When that happens, we praise the client for pushing the designer. Everybody wins!

TL; DR

Research isn't just about setting the project strategy or getting the design just right. In fact, well-rounded research that engages your stakeholders can truly help you run a better project. Do these things to ensure that you're doing right by your team and your stakeholders:

- Understand your project.

    - Goals

    - Stakeholder needs and expectations

    - The makeup of your client's team

    - Any possible issues or risks

- Identify stakeholders and talk about the best times to engage them.

- Participate in stakeholder interviews to gain a well-rounded point of view on the project and its impact on the organization.

- Ask questions that will help you understand any potential issues or risks that may impact your plan.

- Watch out for red flags and resolve issues early on.

CHAPTER 5

Create a Plan

It's always a race to the final deliverable.

The holidays at my house are always festive and hectic. With two young daughters, the anticipation for "THE DAY" to arrive always puts a little extra pressure on us to make sure it's great. Of course, there are 500 steps we need to take leading up to the day: decorating the tree, decorating the house, buying presents, making cookies, and the list goes on. Most importantly, we love to host our family on Christmas Eve. We know that we must have everything done by the time they ring the doorbell because that is truly when the holiday starts.

Last year, we slacked a little and didn't get everything done in time. We had a to-do list about a mile long, and rather than tending to it, we decided to watch Christmas classics and relax. That was a big mistake. By the time Christmas Eve rolled around, we were freaking out, trying to get everything done—picking up last minute gifts, wrapping them, preparing dinner—all of the last minute things we hadn't accounted for. It piled up, and we just weren't ready.

We slapped dinner together and hosted a great party, but our job was not over. We failed to plan our time properly, knowing that the goal was to have everything looking perfect by the time the kids woke up early on Christmas morning. By the time we basically shoved the last family member out of the house, it was game on. We put toys together (while cursing ourselves and the manufacturers), wrapped a bunch of gifts, stuffed stockings, set out cookies and milk . . . and got to bed by 3 a.m. To wake up at 6 a.m.

Had we properly planned what we needed to do from Thanksgiving to December 25, we might not have had such a hard time the night before. Alas, we kicked back and had a good time, and ended up putting ourselves under an immense amount of pressure in the last 24 hours. So typical.

It's also very typical of project work. You've got to have a good plan in place to ensure that you're taking the right steps to meet your project's goals by the established deadline.

Project Plans Will Help You

A project plan is arguably the most important document created on your project. At its core, a plan should communicate your project approach and the process your team will use to manage the project according to scope. If handled with care and great consideration, a good plan should act as an agreement on project objectives, scope, major deliverables, milestones, timing, activities, process, and even resources needed to deliver your product. If you take the time to create a good process around how your plan is built and you consider all of those factors, you can create a great plan that will work for everyone.

Project planning is at the core of what all project managers do, no matter the industry, type of project, or their level of expertise. A project plan defines your approach and the process your team will use to manage the project according to scope. Every project needs a plan: not only does it go a long way toward keeping teams honest in terms of scope and deadlines, but it also communicates vital information to all project stakeholders. If you approach it as something more than a dry document and communicate that aspect of it differently to everyone involved, it can and will be seen as integral to your project's success.

NOTE ON PROCESS

This chapter explores a planning process that works best for traditional projects. If you're working in the Agile approaches, you probably won't need to create plans with the level of fidelity suggested in this chapter.

You could easily slap together a document that shows dates and deliverables, but if you're managing a project that has a hefty budget, lofty goals, and a whole lot of decisions attached to it, you'll find that it's important to take the time to get this document right. With the right amount of background information on your project's scope and requirements, and with a good level of input and collaboration with your team and your clients, you can make a solid, workable plan that will guide everyone through your project. Here's the thing: it doesn't have to be difficult to create.

NOTE FORMATS FOR ALL

Just like projects, project plans come in all shapes, sizes, and formats. Some people like lists with dates, some want a calendar view, and others like Gantt charts. There are several ways to render a plan. Pick the format that will best communicate the details to your team and stakeholders.

The fact is, a plan is more than just dates. It's the story of your project, and you don't want it to be a tall tale! Like any well-written story, there are components that make it good. In fact, any solid plan should answer these questions:

- What are the major deliverables?

- How will you get to those deliverables and the deadline?

- Who is on the project team and what role will they play in those deliverables?

- When will the team meet milestones, and when will other members of the team play a role in contributing to or providing feedback on those deliverables?

Your plan should educate any reviewer—coworkers and clients included—on the logistics of the project. They trust that you've got this, so when reviewing the document, they truly believe that you've considered every possible risk. If you have, it feels good to know that you've done a good job and you're trusted.

Before You Create the Plan

After you've done your own research and you feel that you have acquired all of the possible information about the project that you'll need to craft a plan, it's time to get serious. Chances are, you're feeling fully prepared and ready to dig into the *hows* and *whens* of the project. Well, that's great, because now it's your turn to crank out some work and create a project plan that will impress your team and your clients.

Start with a Sketch

It's so easy to jump right into your project-planning tool of choice to create what looks like a well-thought-out plan. If that's your process, that's fine! Just be sure to think through every possible scenario before you put the time and effort into a formalized document. If you don't, you'll have to go back through your work and make adjustments, and we all know that could end up taking more time than you bargained for. So why not start with a simple sketch to map out and communicate your ideas on process, deliverables, dependencies, and timing? (See Figure 5.1.) It can take you as little as 20 minutes and will sell your ideas to your team before delivering something that feels "written in stone."

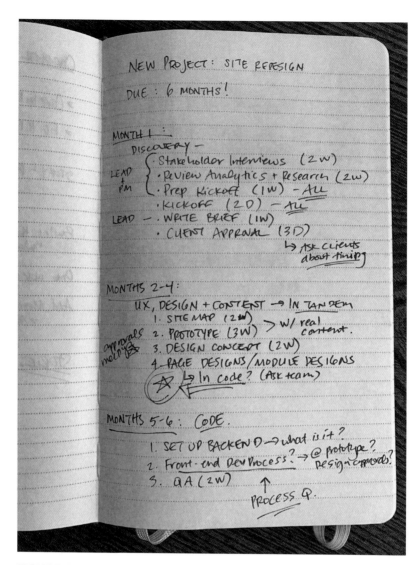

FIGURE 5.1

Sketching your ideas first will help determine deliverables, process, timing, and constraints. Do this before jumping into a tool, because it's quick.

Grab a pen and a notebook, or stand in front of a whiteboard and sketch out your ideas. Feeling overwhelmed, or don't know where to start? Take a look at your scope document. Does it outline specific deliverables or timing? Refer back to your meeting notes. When you asked your clients all those questions, did any specific process tweaks come up? Are there dates or events you need to keep in mind?

If this is new to you, you can feel slightly lost, but it's important to remember that the tool you put the plan in won't do the thinking for you. You control the process, and you can craft a plan without any tool at all. Just keep the following factors in mind.

An Overall Approach to the Project

What's the first deliverable? What comes after that? How do those deliverables help you get to the end goal? Does your team prefer to work within the framework of a mindset like Agile? What are the frameworks that you can apply to this project, given the variables you discovered in your pre-project client Q&A?

The Tasks That Will Need to Be Completed

Don't think about your project in phases. Think about deliverables and the value that each of them provides. For instance, if you're delivering a design concept, what work needs to be done before that can begin, and what work can happen when it's approved—or concurrently? Knowing about each task and planning its dependencies will help you string everything together.

The Roles or People Who Will Work on the Project

Who's on your project team and what do they do? Also, how can you leverage their expertise and collaboration to get things done more efficiently? If you have an idea of how your team could work together and present ideas to them, they're going to be more open to discussing the process and coming up with ideas on how to approach the project together. If you harness the power of team collaboration before your work starts, you'll find that the work product will be stronger and the team will be happier. Using a RACI matrix might help you here. Check out Chapter 9, "Setting and Managing Expectations," for details on how to set up and use one.

You'll also want to keep resourcing in mind. If your organization allows people to be on more than one project at a time, it can potentially cause conflicts on your project. That's a headache you'll want to avoid. Be sure to review resourcing plans and ensure that your team is available to conduct the work on your project over the course of time you're estimating.

The Time You and Your Team Need to Execute Work

Be honest about the time your team will need to get their work done. Don't forget to look back at your project estimate (if you have one) to see how many hours were scoped for tasks. This can be a huge help in determining timelines. Of course, there are other things to consider as well.

Other Project Work

If you're working on a team of people who are working on multiple projects and have everyday operations tasks to manage, you're going to want to have a complete picture of each person's availability. If they are responsible for other projects, you'll want to discuss key dates to avoid so that you don't make the mistake of double-booking (and stressing out/upsetting) your team.

Client Reviews and Approvals

This is the ultimate project curveball. You must account for enough time for your clients to review, discuss, and approve deliverables. But is that time going to be the same for every deliverable? Once you've had the conversation about who will make decisions and who will be involved on the project, think through the deliverables and how long you'd estimate your clients should take. Be generous with that time at first and see if you can negotiate any time back when you review the final plan with your clients.

Dates

Your plan will crumble as soon as you hit a date that doesn't work for your team or your clients. Check schedules on both sides of the fence and be sure to account for holidays, closings, vacations, meetings, and any other possible date that could cause outages. If you get ahead of that kind of information before you commit to a plan, you won't have to freak out about delays and risks due to a missed meeting or deadline.

Get Realistic About Timing: Break Down Tasks

Having a hard time sorting out how long it will take you to get a task done? Try a work breakdown structure, a fixture in classic project management methodology and systems engineering that breaks a project task into smaller components. Creating a work breakdown structure for any plan or set of tasks helps you get granular about the work that needs to be done on any given project. Check out this sample work breakdown structure for creating the wireframes for the Gantt Museum website redesign project (see Figure 5.2).

WORK BREAKDOWN STRUCTURE:
WIREFRAMES

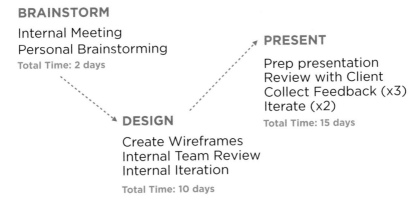

BRAINSTORM

Internal Meeting
Personal Brainstorming

Total Time: 2 days

PRESENT

Prep presentation
Review with Client
Collect Feedback (x3)
Iterate (x2)

Total Time: 15 days

DESIGN

Create Wireframes
Internal Team Review
Internal Iteration

Total Time: 10 days

FIGURE 5.2

Try this version of a work breakdown structure by simply listing tasks and subtasks.

The Benefits of the Work Breakdown Structure

In Chapter 3, "Start with an Estimate," we talked about the WBS in terms of estimating. You should be able to apply the same methodology when planning, and it will help do the following:

- Be granular quickly and create a simple time estimate.

- Confirm steps with your team in an easily digestible way.

- Create to-do lists related to tasks.

- Create a detailed view that will educate your client on the effort involved with any task.

- Create templates for similar projects or tasks.

It's All in the Assumptions

When you're working on a draft plan, you'll probably make some assumptions about the way things will go. These could be details about the overall process, who's doing the work, your internal process, feedback timing, and so on. As you're sketching, be sure to list those assumptions. This will help you remember all of those details when you discuss the plan with your team. If you've got a list of assumptions in front of you, you can confirm or change them when you're confirming the plan.

What's It Look Like?

Presentation is everything, at least that's what our designer friends say. But it's true—you need to be proud of the way your plan looks! Maybe it's a Gantt chart, maybe it's a calendar, or even a line-by-line masterpiece. No matter how you're doing it, you should know the fundamentals of using your plan to its fullest and how to communicate its most important points. The way your plan looks should be secondary to the points you need to convey with it. The way it functions, however, can matter, especially if you want to be able to respond to and project the impact of changes. If it is overly manual, then updating it and managing it for changes will be very time consuming, especially if it is detailed.

> **NOTE** GETTING GANTT-Y
>
> Wondering what a Gantt chart is? Well, it's a chart in which a series of horizontal lines show the amount of work done or production completed in certain periods of time in relation to the amount planned for those periods. Looking for an easy way to create Gantt charts? Try TeamGantt: **teamgantt.com**.

Get Buy-in Early

As soon as you're comfortable with your plan, take some time to review it (and all of those assumptions) with your team. It can be a short, relaxed meeting to work out the overall process, deliverables, responsibilities, timing, and anything else under the sun that could impact the success of the project. As a team, you should be able to agree on what's going to work. When you have everyone's buy-in on the overall approach, you'll be one step closer to having a plan that not only looks great, but will also feel appropriate and workable.

Formalize Your Plan

After you've sketched your plan and confirmed the most important process details, you're on your way to putting it into a digital format. Working in the project planning tool of your choice to lay out timing, tasks, dependencies, and so on will make the plan easy to read and update. While this work is easy, there are some things you should do to make your plan readable.

1. **Enter tasks in groups.**

   Creating groups of tasks will make your plan easier to read, and it will allow your readers to see which tasks are part of a deliverable or a phase (see Figure 5.3).

2. **Get granular with tasks.**

   The more detail you can spell out when it comes to tasks, the better you will be able to track your progress and the steps leading up to a deliverable. Refer back to your work breakdown structure and list the steps you used to create that.

The Gantt Museum Website Redesign

▶ Project Research & Discovery

▶ Project Brief and Project Plan

▼ UX Design

  ▼ Site Map

    PT: Create v1 Site Map

    PT: Present v1 Site Map

    GM: Provide Feedback

    PT: Deliver v2 Site Map for approval

    GM: Approve Site Map

  ▼ Wireframes

    PT: Deliver v1 Wireframes

    PT: Present v1 Wireframes

    GM: Provide Feedback

    PT: Deliver v2 Wireframes

    GM: Provide Feedback

    PT: Deliver v3 Wireframes

    GM: Approve Wireframes

  ▼ Content Strategy

    PT: Deliver Initial CS Recommendations

    GM: Provide Feedback

    PT: Ongoing Content Development and Review

FIGURE 5.3

Breaking parts of your project into groups will help you keep track of tasks by phase and deliverable, and it makes scanning a long document much easier.

3. **Identify responsible parties (company, people).**

   Identifying which company is responsible for each task will help your readers seek out their tasks more easily (see Figure 5.4). When creating a task, you can put the company name (or an acronym) in front of the task. You'll also want to take that a step further and assign a responsible person for each task. This will help you with resource planning and accountability.

FIGURE 5.4
Use company or individual initials to call out responsibility in your plan.

| PT: Design concepts |
| PT: Present concepts |
| GM: Provide feedback |
| PT: Deliver revised concepts |
| GM: Provide feedback |
| PT: Deliver final concept |
| GM: Approve design concept |

4. **Be sure to display start and end dates for each task.**

   Seems like a silly tip, but it's easy to hide this info in some apps! Regardless of what tool you're using, you'll want to make it clear not only when a task ends, but also when it starts (see Figure 5.5). Again, this will help to keep your team and clients accountable.

▼ Wireframes	0%			
PT: Deliver v1 Wireframes	0%		7/22/15	7/28/15
PT: Present v1 Wireframes	0%		7/29/15	7/29/15
GM: Provide Feedback	0%		7/30/15	8/3/15
PT: Deliver v2 Wireframes	0%		8/4/15	8/7/15
GM: Provide Feedback	0%		8/10/15	8/11/15
PT: Deliver v3 Wireframes	0%		8/12/15	8/14/15
GM: Approve Wireframes	☐	◇	8/17/15	8/17/15
▼ Content Strategy	0%			
PT: Deliver Initial CS Recommendations	0%		7/27/15	7/31/15
GM: Provide Feedback	0%		8/3/15	8/7/15
PT: Ongoing Content Development and Review	0%		7/6/15	8/17/15

FIGURE 5.5
Showing start and end dates in a plan leaves no question as to when something should be worked on or is due.

5. **Account for time off and holidays.**

   Now is your chance to block time off in your plan. This is important now, because as soon as your timeline shifts (you know it will, don't fight it), you'll open yourself up to making an error and dropping a deadline on a date that should be blocked. If you note them in your plan, that won't happen.

6. **Note dependencies.**

   If you're not going to move forward on the project without an approval, or one task must be done before another, now is your chance to note it (see Figure 5.6). Not every planning tool offers dependency functionality, and it can be a huge help. As your plan shifts, the flow of the work will stay intact.

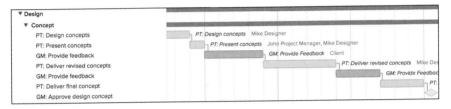

FIGURE 5.6

Noting dependencies in your Gantt chart or notes can help your team and stakeholders know what must be completed to proceed with the following tasks.

7. **Use the "notes" field to capture details.**

   Sometimes your team and clients forget what they committed to, or maybe they don't fully understand the intent of a task or group. Use the notes section of your plan to spell things out.

8. **Check team availability.**

   If you're lucky enough to use a product that shows your overall team availability, you'd better use it! Knowing how your team is booked and what projects they are part of will play a huge role in how on-time your project will be. Having an overall view of their time available and conflicting work will help you adjust your plan to either meet the needs of existing project work or shift the milestones you've put in your plan.

Double-Check Your Work

Creating a project plan is just like writing an article, creating a design, or building a bike. You want to be sure you get it right before it's read, viewed, or used. If you deliver a plan that has a mistake, misinterprets a task, or even misses a date, you'll end up looking bad. People lose faith in project managers easily, so you must be diligent about the quality of your work. Grab your teammates and ask them to review the plan before you post it for review.

Of course, you'll also want to be ready to get some feedback on your plan. Formalizing a plan means that you're taking a set of ideas and expanding on them. That also means that you might interpret something differently than a teammate. That's OK! If you set up your plan using the guidelines in this chapter, you'll have an easy time of managing and updating.

Get Plan Buy-in

The first version of your plan will not be the final one. In fact, any good plan will be flexible enough to be updated and changed easily. So before you try to commit it to project history, be sure to understand that you've got some work ahead of you. First, you'll want to confirm your plan with your team and make the necessary updates; then you'll want to review it with your clients. From there, you'll manage your plan and make updates as the project dictates. Use the advice in this chapter to "baseline" and manage your plan through the course of your project.

Make It Readable

There is no doubt that reading a project plan can be boring. In order to stop your dear readers from skimming your work of art, use some formatting skills to make sure that tasks, durations, milestones and dates are crystal clear. No matter what tool you're using, you should be able to do these things:

- Include all pertinent project info:
  - Client name, project name
  - Version number, delivery date

- Break out milestones and deliverables in sections by creating headers and indenting subsequent tasks. (Reading one long list of tasks is really monotonous and can be mind-numbing even to the best of us.)

- Call out which team is responsible for each task (example: "CLIENT: Provide feedback").

- Add resources responsible for each task so there is no confusion about who is responsible for what.

- Be sure to show durations of tasks clearly. Each task should have a start and end date.

- Add notes to tasks that might seem confusing or need explanation. It never hurts to add detail!

- Call out project dependencies. These are important when you're planning for the risk of delays.

Include your company's logo and your client's logo if you're feeling fancy. Use your company's branded fonts if you're feeling really fancy.

In addition to all of this, you should be as flexible as possible when it comes to how your plan is presented. There is no absolute when it comes to how you represent your plan as long as you and your team understand what goes into it. Remember, people absorb information differently. While some people prefer a list view, others might prefer to see a calendar or even a Gantt chart. You can make all of those variations work if you've taken the steps to create a solid plan.

Step 1: Team Review

If you followed the steps presented in Chapter 3, you discussed your plan at a high level. You determined overall process, deliverables, and assignments as a group and agreed to the way things should work—all based on a high-level sketch. Then you created a detailed plan that outlined the specifics: phases, tasks, deliverables, due dates, dependencies, and resourcing. You put a lot of thought into how the high-level plan could be executed on a day-to-day basis.

That means that some of the details you discussed about the high-level plan may have shifted when you formalized the ideas with real dates and restrictions. This is completely normal—you have to get specific about things like deadlines, working time, resourcing and other project work, and the time your clients need on projects.

So what do you do when you see those shifts happen? Whether they change or not, you have to take the formal plan back to your team to review. If you don't, you run the risk of someone not agreeing to a new detail or date, and that will cause frustration on the project. Follow these steps for a thorough review process that will get your team aligned on the plan:

1. **Make a copy or send access to the plan to each of your team members.**

    Or post physical copies in a place where your team and stake-holders can always see them—like in a project war room, a team space, or even the lunchroom. You want them to see the new plan and have access to it at all times. Keeping your plan in an accessible place means that everyone is accountable not only for reviewing and confirming it initially, but also for checking in on it as the project progresses.

2. **When sharing your plan, reiterate the overall process.**

    Go over where you'll start (and what the immediate next steps will be), the key dependencies, major meetings, holidays blocked, and, of course, the deadline. At the same time, be sure to note any major differences in the new, formalized plan. Explain why any details may have shifted in this version and be open to alternate approaches. Showing your team that you're not trying to control the process and plan will build a collaborative team atmosphere, and it will show them that you're there to facilitate a great process.

3. **Give the team some time to review the plan individually and schedule a short meeting to go over the specifics in detail in person.**

    Allowing them time to review the document on their own ensures that you can keep the meeting short.

4. **In your meeting, reiterate what you emailed.**

    If you see issues with this version or anticipate any confusion, address those immediately. This is your chance to present the plan and explain why you've made certain decisions or explain any decisions that might make you slightly uncomfortable. After all, you should be assessing the plan for risk from day one. If everything seems too perfect, you might want to think about it a little further. No plan exists without some sort of risk or potential issue. From there, open it up to conversation. Because this plan is based on an earlier agreement, you should be able to do this meeting within 30 minutes. Or, if the project is short enough and the plan is very straightforward, you might even skip this step altogether.

5. **After your meeting, make the adjustments needed and check the final version.**

   Make sure that you're comfortable with it and post it for your team to review. This time around, feel free to give your team a short review time so you can speed up the process. The last thing you want is for your team to think they are being bogged down by the project management process. But, it's also important they know that they're just as accountable for the plan as you are.

Now you're one step closer to confirming your plan and getting things underway.

Step 2: Client/Stakeholder Review

When you're working on a project with a client or even a product owner, it's critical to be 100 percent sure they understand all of the details your team has discussed. Remember, your clients may not be familiar with your process or deliverables so this is your chance to enlighten them. You may want to send the document to them in advance, but be sure to set up a call or an in-person meeting to review the plan in detail. Chances are, they will be confused by what they're looking at, so you'll want to take the opportunity to review it line-by-line. This may sound painful, but it's an important step in ensuring that you're in agreement not only on timing, but also on how you'll deliver the final product. Use the initial review of your plan as your chance to explain.

Process

Explain your overall process and how you, as a team, arrived at the approach. Feel free to explain how it has worked on previous projects, or how you're trying something new. You also might want to talk about ways the process might change during the project. Cover all of your bases and set the right expectations. No matter what, stand behind the approach and be confident about its potential for success.

Deliverables

Review the deliverables and all of the details that will help you, as a team, produce your project on time. It's important to explain what work must be done to complete a deliverable, and why it will take the time you have allotted. If you explain these details now, your clients will not push for unrealistic deadlines. And if your plan shows tasks, your client will understand just how much work is being done.

While reviewing your plan, your client may have questions about what a deliverable is and what it does. This is great, because it means they are engaged in the process and look forward to seeing what the team will deliver. If you can, share some similar documents or deliverables from other projects and explain what they are intended to do (and not do) and how they relate to other project deliverables and decisions. The more you can educate your clients early on, the easier time your team will have at winning them over when presenting your work. After all, a client who is invested in and truly understands your work is not just a client—they are a partner.

At the same time, you should set expectations for your deliverable review processes. In your plan, you've probably made some estimates based on the amount of time your clients will need to review your work as a team and provide feedback. If you've had conversations with your clients early in the process, you know how much time they need. This is your chance to point back to that conversation and tell them the timing is based on that discussion, but if that is no longer the case, this is the time to make adjustments. At this point, you want to be as realistic as possible about how the project will go. There's nothing worse than changing the review process—or the people involved—midstream on a project. Explain this to your clients, and they will think twice about timing and what is realistic for them. And when they see the time they need in relation to the time you're taking, as well as the deadline, they will most likely be motivated to work hard to meet their dates.

Don't forget to point out dependencies. If your client misses their deadline, what will that do to the project? Where can you be flexible, and what makes you nervous? Put it all on the table now and document it in meeting notes so that everyone is aware of the potential issues you're spotting early on.

It's never just about the work—it's about the people who are doing the work. Be sure to communicate the fact that the team has reviewed the plan and mention some of the items you discussed as a team and how you arrived at some decisions. There's a lot of value in showing your clients the human side of your process and your team, because it's often easy for them to think of you as a "shop" that just gets the work done. They don't know all of the details, and maybe they don't want to. But if you share some details about who's doing what, and any other key things they're working on, it will help them relate to it a bit more.

It can be tricky talking to clients about other work you're doing, but it shouldn't be. The fact is, you're a business and you have other clients and projects. Show your clients the fact that you take great care to schedule your time and projects in a way that works for you and for them. If you're really good at this, you'll have scheduled your project around others, and there will be a little bit of a cushion in your timing to make future shifts. Even if that isn't the case, it would not be a terrible idea to set the expectation that a one-day delay on your client's side may not equate to a one-day delay on your side. Simply let your clients know that their plan is crafted around others and a carefully crafted resourcing plan will help them understand the importance of sticking to the dates and process you've outlined.

Step 3: Confirm Everything

You've put a heck of a lot of work into creating this plan, so talking through the details to make sure that everyone is comfortable with it should be pretty important to you. If this means giving your client and team some extra time to think things through on their own, so be it. Of course, you never want this process to take so much time that it delays any of the project work. You can create the plan while work is underway—but don't let it go unconfirmed for too long. You want to be sure that you have an agreement, because the details in your plan will dictate so much, including your immediate next steps.

Step 4: Manage and Update

Just because you've confirmed your plan does not mean that you're done with it! In fact, you'll find that your plan is a living and breathing document. At a minimum, you should update the "Percent Complete" column on your project on a daily or weekly basis.

It's gratifying to see that number go up! Plus, the chances that you'll have to make adjustments here or there are pretty significant. It's not common for every project to stick to its plan 100 percent of the time. Life happens, ideas change processes, deadlines are missed, and plans change. That may mean that your deadline has to shift, or maybe your process will no longer work for the project. As long as you are flexible and can adapt to the revolving door of changes, so can your project plan.

It's really easy to be frustrated by a change in plans. Don't let it get to you—remember that you've got a team who has already committed to coming up with a plan that works and a client whom you've educated on your process and deliverables. You've done a lot of work to get these people on board with the plan, and they're now invested enough in the plan and the project so they'll be willing to help make adjustments or think through new ways of working if needed.

Be sure to provide updates to your team and your clients as plans change—or stay on track. Keep your plan in an accessible place, but communicate how things are going based on the plan. For every change to the plan, there's a cause. You usually either make a change because you're adding more value or because a specific task was not executed according to the plan. In the first case, you need to explain the trade-off to everyone. In the second case, you need to understand the implications of the change as soon as humanly possible and work to minimize it. You'll always end up on top if you've communicated or resolved an issue early on or even paid a compliment on a job well done.

> **NOTE** **ORGANIZE YOUR NOTES**
>
> Wondering how to categorize all of these random notes and ideas? Make a running list of issues, questions, risks, and ideas. Categorize them by topic and address them one by one.

What You Really Need to Know

Quite often, you'll receive a tome of project details. Pages upon pages of requirements, team biographies, invoicing instructions, contractual clauses, and the like. It's very critical that you read through all of that documentation. But when it comes to creating a plan, this is what you need to know, no matter what type of project you're managing.

Project goals:

- The client or team's intended process or methodology

- The team and their expertise

- Expectations on deliverables

- Expectations on iteration and collaboration when creating and revising deliverables

- Who the client stakeholder team is, and specifically who the main decision makers are

- The amount of time the client will need to review work and provide feedback

- Dependencies

- Deadlines

Never leave any of these items unanswered. If you're responsible for creating the project plan that means that you must be sure that all factors have been considered. If you don't, the project will definitely hit a bump in the road and every finger will be pointed at you. For instance, if you have not fully explored the decision-making process, there is a great chance that you'll encounter the good old "swoop and poop" during the process. If you don't know what that is, it's when a stakeholder you weren't aware of swoops into the project at the 11th hour and poops on the work—and puts you back at square one. It's a budget and timeline nightmare that will become a reality if you don't practice your due diligence.

> **NOTE** **DON'T SKIP THE DOCUMENTATION**
>
> It's best to sift through documentation away from your desk, or at your desk with all of your favorite apps closed. Get some alone time with that document. Read it thoroughly and make notes on the things that are red flags, questions, risks, or discussion points in the document. This will ensure that you're not missing any potential risks.

Just remember, you can get as much info as possible, and details can change. Do your best to document the information you have so that you can account for it in your plan. The next chapter will present ways you can dig deeper to create a plan that will work for you.

Sample Project and Plan

The best way to illustrate best practices for creating a project plan is to actually show you an example of a well-done plan! The example included here (see Figure 5.7) is of a website redesign, so if digital PM is your thing, you will get it immediately. If your background is non-digital by nature,

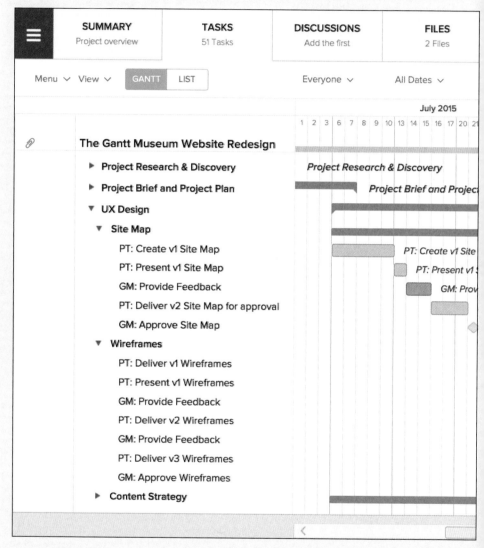

FIGURE 5.7

Want to see the whole sample plan? Visit **brettharned.com/resources**.

that's just fine! There's enough guidance here for you to apply the principles presented to your own projects. Look at the language, structure, and timing used and you'll pick up what you need. Plus, you might learn a thing or two about what it takes to build a website.

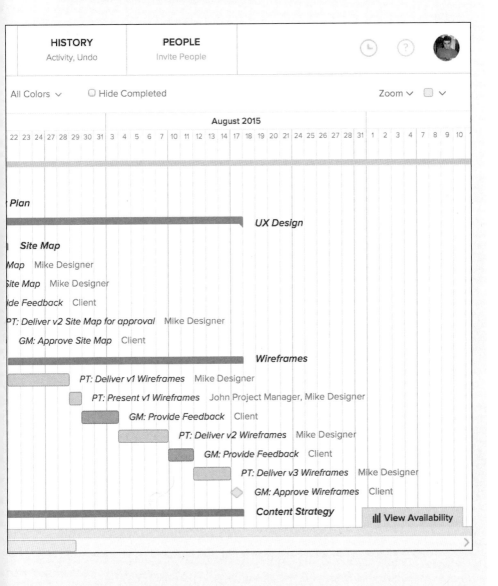

Get Planning

Sometimes projects are smooth and alarmingly easy to manage, and sometimes they are a complete nightmare that wakes you up at 3 a.m. every other night (it happens). Regardless, plans will change. With a good team and a clear scope of work, you're on your way to making a solid plan that is manageable and well-thought-out. In the end, having a solid plan is your best defense against project chaos.

Not all projects or processes are the same. In fact, some processes call for a more open, flexible way of project planning. If your team and your clients are happy with less detail, then you should absolutely work that way. Maybe this full planning process won't work for your organization—and that is OK. The goal here is for you to understand that the core principle of planning and managing a project is through good communication tactics. One of those tactics is a well-crafted project plan that has been reviewed and discussed by all parties involved in the project. If that plan ends up being a simple sketch, a Kanban board, or a daily stand-up meeting, you're doing it right!

NOTE THE LIVING DOCUMENT

Just because you create a plan in the beginning of a project doesn't mean that you're done with it. In fact, your project plan is a document that you and your team should review regularly, especially when working on large projects. As the PM, you should check in at least a few times per week. Just to make sure your team is paying attention, you might want to schedule review meetings to review and validate the plan.

TL; DR

Projects come in all shapes and sizes, but they all require you to track the details: process, tasks, people, decisions, dependencies, and more. In order to make sense of the chaos, you should:

- Sketch a draft plan to share with your team.

- Discuss the draft plan and answer your questions on process, tasks, pacing, timelines, and responsibilities.

- Formalize your plan in a project-planning tool.

- Get buy-in from your team and your stakeholders.

- Manage and update the plan regularly.

CHAPTER 6

Managing Resources

*Staffing teams can feel a bit like a game of Tetris,
but don't forget your teams are human beings.
They have interests, strengths, and qualities that
should be considered above their availability.*

I loved the game *Tetris* as a kid. I played the Game Boy version for hours. It's easy to get wrapped up in the concept of little shapes coming together in a logical way to clear a goal. The pieces complement one another, yet they all naturally work in different ways. The game has stuck with me since I was a kid (and, no, I'm not a gamer). I now have it on my phone and iPad and find myself playing it when I'm on a flight or bored, waiting for something to happen (which is never these days). Whether I'm playing the game a lot or not, the idea of making tiny boxes fit in neatly and clearing out rows of work is ingrained in my brain. It's the project manager in me.

But here's the thing: What project managers do on a daily basis when it comes to managing resources or staffing is similar to *Tetris*, and it's a big project management challenge that we all face. The biggest difference between resourcing and *Tetris*? The team members we're trying to assign tasks to aren't blocks. They're human beings, and they need to be treated as such.

NOTE YOUR TEAM ARE PEOPLE, TOO!

Let's move away from calling people "resources," please. We're really just staffing projects or assigning tasks. We're not using people to *just* get things done. We're asking them to solve challenges that are presented in our projects.

Set the Stage for Organized Resource Planning

The challenge of managing a team is making sure that they stay busy and working on tasks, yet are not completely overbooked. It's a difficult balance to find, particularly when your projects require a variety of skills at different times, which seem to change all too often.

At the most basic level, you want to set up a system for tracking your projects and your team members' time on those projects (see Figure 6.1). A simple goal is to ensure that you can confidently commit to deadlines on projects with the knowledge that your team is actually available to do the related work. It seems like a simple goal, but it's often a difficult one to keep up with due to changes on projects, changes in personal schedules (hey, life happens), and an influx of new work and requests. But it's not an insurmountable challenge.

In fact, a simple spreadsheet could help you, particularly if you're managing a smaller team. At the core, you want to track these items:

- **Projects:** List them all, even the non-billable ones, or the other things that aren't projects but end up taking a lot of time—like business development.

- **People:** List every person you work with.

- **Estimated time:** Track hours, days, weeks, etc. Make your best guess—based on your timeline or calendar—on how much each person will spend on a project or a task.

Week of 5/22	Sid Estimate	Nancy Estimate	Johnny Estimate	Malcolm Estimate
Project X	8	10		16
Project A	20		24	8
Internal Project	2	12	4	20
Admin Time	8	8	8	8
Time Off	4			
Weekly Total	42	30	36	52
Available Hours	-2	10	4	-12

FIGURE 6.1

Use a Google Spreadsheet, Numbers, or Excel to input your project and team data.

A couple of notes on how to use a spreadsheet to forecast team availability:

- This should be set up on a week-by-week basis to minimize confusion. (Use tabs in your spreadsheet for each new week.)

- Always consider the "nonbillable" things that people must do (like stand-up meetings, internal tasks, sales, etc.).

- The final cell contains a formula that tallies the hours for you; if the hours go over your typical limit (think of a 40-hour work week), it will turn red to notify you. You'll want to have a good idea for just how "utilized" someone should be (32 hours/week is usually a good target).

- You can input the actual hours logged in your time tracking system if you'd like. It could help with future estimating. (If you're not tracking time, check in with your team on time percentages to get a gut check.)

- Check your estimates with your team to make sure that the hours actually align with their assessment of the task. (This might help with avoiding that red number!)

- Communicate these hours to the entire team each week. Making sure that everyone "is in the know" will help on *any* project. Discussing it with individuals will help you understand effort, blockers, and possibly even different ways of working.

> **NOTE** TOOLS
>
> The landscape for project management tools is changing constantly. There are a number of tools in the marketplace for helping you manage and communicate this data. If you're working with a team of 10 or more, you might want to abandon the spreadsheet approach for something more official, organized, and supported. Bonus: Many of these tools handle more than just resourcing!

Here's the thing—it's not just about numbers. The issue that makes estimating a team's project hours difficult is that everyone works differently. There is no way to standardize the human factor here, and that's what makes it tough. Forget the fact that no one on your team is a robot, and they all work at their own pace. Think about sick days, vacations, client delays, changes on projects, and so on. It's a never-ending flow of shapes that must fit into the box that is a project. Be sure to have an ongoing dialogue about your staffing plans and challenges.

Match Resource Skills to Projects

Projects only slow down when decisions are not made. In that magical moment when things are actually going well, you want to make sure that your team can continue the pace. The only way to do that is by connecting with your team and understanding what motivates them. Here are some things to consider:

- **Interests:** If you have a team member who loves beer, why not put that person on the beer design site? Maybe you have multiple people who want to be on the project, but they are all busy on other projects. These are the breaks. You've got to do what is right for the company and your budget. If you can put interests first, it's awesome. It won't always work out that way for everyone, but it's a good first step to try.

- **Skill sets:** It's as simple as getting to know each and every team member's work. Some people are meant to create specific types of designs or experiences. It not only has to do with interests, but it also has to do with strengths within those tasks. Sure, I may love beer, but that doesn't mean that I am meant to design the site that caters to the audience the client is trying to reach.

- **Moving schedules:** Projects will always change. One week you know you're working against a firm deadline, and the next week that has changed due to the clients, the needs of the project, or some other reason someone conjured up. It's tough to know when that change will happen, but when it does, how you'll fill someone's time with other work should be high on your mind.

- **Holidays:** People always extend them. Plan for that!

- **Vacations:** It's great to know about these in advance. Be sure you know your company's policies around vacations. You never ever want to be the PM who says "Well, you have a deadline on X date and that will conflict with your very expensive/exciting trip, so, um...no." Ask people to request trips at least a month in advance so that you can plan ahead and make it work.

- **Illness:** We are all humans and that means we're fine one day and bedridden the next. You've always got to be ready for a back-up plan. It shouldn't fall on your client stakeholders to make up time, but sometimes it has to. Or sometimes you need to look for someone to pitch in on intermediate tasks to keep things on track while your "rock star" or "ninja" is getting better.

NOTE ALIGN PLANS WITH STAFFING

When you're working hard to keep up with staffing plans, you've got to have updated project plans. A small change in a plan could cause a change in staffing—even by a few hours—and throw everything else off.

Save Yourself and Your Team from Burnout

If you're busy and not slowing down any time soon, you want to keep this spreadsheet (or tool) updated often. If you're working at an agency, knowing what's in your pipeline can also help you. Stay aligned with the person in charge of sales or assigning new projects so that you can anticipate upcoming needs and timelines. In some cases, you may even want to put some basic data in your spreadsheet or tool so that you can anticipate needs.

> **NOTE** GOOD RESOURCING CAN JUSTIFY MORE HELP
>
> The value of tracking this data goes beyond your projects. It can help business owners make important decisions on growing a company.

No matter what you do, be sure to communicate about staffing as much as possible. If you're in an organization that is constantly handling change, you'll know that it's a tough target to hit. In fact, your numbers will often be slightly off, but you'll find comfort in knowing that you're doing everything you can to stay ahead of the resource crunch. At the same time, your team will appreciate that you're doing everything you can to protect their work-life balance.

Stakeholders Are Resources, Too

When you're working on a team with a project, you have to consider the stakeholders as decision makers, too. Let's face it—no one has ever been trained to be a good client, stakeholder, or project sponsor. In addition to that, they are likely to be working on several projects with several people at one time. Life as a client can be hectic! So do everything you can to help them plan their time appropriately. In general, you should let the stakeholders know they'll have to plan for these things:

- **Meetings:** You'll conduct a kickoff meeting, weekly status updates, deliverable reviews, etc.

- **Scheduling:** You'll need stakeholders to wrangle calendars to get folks into said meetings.

- **Gathering feedback:** This sounds easy, but it is not. You will need this person to spend time with all of the stakeholders to get their feedback and collate it for you to make sure there are no conflicting opinions.

- **Chasing down decisions:** There are points on every project where one person will need to make sure there is agreement and decisions can be made to keep the project moving.

- **Daily ad hoc email, phone calls:** Questions and requests will pop up, and you'll need timely responses.

- **Operations:** You might need invoices to be reviewed and approved or change requests to be reviewed and discussed. The stakeholders will need to make time to operate the project from their side of things.

This is a lot of work. And just like PM work, it is very hard to quantify or plan. If you're in good hands, you're working with someone who has good PM skills. If not, give them the list above along with a copy of this book. But seriously, if you can assist them with planning their time, it might be as simple as including action items or to-dos for them in a weekly email or in your status report. Just remember, they are busy and want the project to run smoothly as well. Help them make that happen.

TL; DR

Managing projects is hard enough, but being the person to manage who works on what and when can be even more difficult. However, if you don't keep track of this basic information, you'll likely find it hard to meet deadlines and wrap up projects without major issues. Here are some simple things you can do to make sure that your team stays busy, yet not completely overbooked:

- Set up a simple spreadsheet to forecast projects and hours per team member.

  - This data should be based on what's included in your project scopes and timelines—be sure to double-check that.

  - You may want to check out one of the resourcing tools that are out there now.

- Be sure to account for a number of factors that you can't necessarily control in this process—for example, interests, skill sets, moving schedules, holidays, vacations, and so on.

- Account for your sales process if you're in an agency and stay ahead of new project requests.

- Remember that you're dealing with people here.

CHAPTER 7

Communicate Like a Pro

Being a clear communicator when you're nervous or your emotions are running high can be tough.

I played baseball, soccer, and basketball from my toddler days up until high school. In my freshman year of high school, I decided to give football a go. (I was asked to give it a shot, because as a big guy, they figured I would be good.) So I gave it a shot. And man, was that eye-opening. Immediately, I noticed an intense shift in the way I was talked to (or at). Coaches and assistants barked orders. They were aggressive. It wasn't for me, but I stuck with it for as long as I could (three weeks).

Upon deciding to leave the team, I felt as though I needed to have a one-on-one conversation with the coach to explain why. Looking back, that was very adult of me. But the words that came out of my mouth were far more mature than I think I would have expected. I told him the reason I couldn't stay on the team had nothing to do with my ability or my interest in the sport. It was about the way I was constantly barked at—even when things were good. I told him that I'd been playing sports for the better part of my life, and I always enjoyed them. But this? This wasn't fun for me. I also explained that I knew it was the norm, but that it never made me feel like I was a part of a team. It never gave me a great feeling. After spitting that out, I expected to be yelled at, told to leave.

But it didn't happen.

The coach told me that he understood, and that it wasn't for everyone. His coaching tactics were rooted in his experiences as an athlete, and they worked for him. Also, he couldn't change the way he coached for one person, so there was nothing he could do. That was fine with me—I didn't want special attention. I just wanted him to know why I was quitting...because I'd never been a quitter.

That night, I lay in bed thinking about how things could have been different had I just sucked it up, *or* had the coach taken the message and changed his approach. I probably would have a Heisman trophy on my desk right now. No, but seriously, it might have changed my high school and college careers. Before falling asleep, I thought, "Who cares? I'm owning this change, and I'm making my own decisions based on what will make me happy and not stress me out." I was proud that I had the guts to talk to the coach and to question the way I was being communicated to. It left an impression on me. It taught me that I needed to consider the way I communicate with others in any situation. It prepared me for my career long before I had one.

• • •

Imagine managing a project without any form of communication. Unless you're producing something on your own for yourself, it would be wholly impossible. That's because projects are often complicated with various layers of details, requirements, and decisions. Each step requires a new task to discuss, because it's dependent on another task or decision—or even another person. Sure, you can make it so that all of those decisions are funneled through your favorite project management planning tool, but just a plan or a tool won't help you complete a project successfully. You've got to use your most basic human skills to manage a project: communications. And it's not just about the words coming out of your mouth or the words you type in a message. It's about intent, tone, openness, and general comfort with the work and the people around you. It's not easy, but you can do it. It's very important to remember that no matter what role you're playing on a project, if you're not making a strong effort to communicate with your team, you will likely fail.

Solid Communications Earn Trust

The foundation of good project communications starts with building trust among your team and stakeholders. The best way to get to a place where everyone is trusted and respected is by being honest. That's right, drop your guard and recognize that hiding mistakes, ideas that could put you over scope, awkward client conversations, or whatever else that gives you the project heebee-jeebees will never be good for the team or the project. Earn trust by simply sharing important project details and conversations in the open. At the same time, take time to form relationships with your team and stakeholders. This can be done through conversations or interactions that not only focus on the project, its goals, and how you'll work together to meet them, but also about yourselves.

It's critical for project managers to make time to interact with their teams about nonproject things. That's right—get personal. Tell jokes. Have some fun. Talk about your interests, your home life—anything that will help you find common ground with your team. You'll want to do that at appropriate times and be sure that personal conversations don't get in the way of your work. After all, you're there to work. But it's the little interactions that set the tone for how you'll work together, and more importantly, how you as the PM are deeply interested not only in the project logistics, but also the people involved. After all, they're going to help you deliver a successful project. And as soon as those relationships are built, it's immensely easier to ask for things, have difficult conversations, and guide the project to success.

> **NOTE** WATCH YOUR TONE
>
> The most difficult part about written conversations is getting the tone right. It's very easy to be direct, but it's just as easy to come off as a jerk. If you're feeling like you can't get it right and don't want to upset someone, ask a friend or colleague to review your message for you before sending it out. Call it a "tone check."

It's Not About You

Remember, it's not all about you and your process as the PM. It is all about you working with the team to come up with a structure that works for *everyone*. You may ask: why change your communication strategy from project to project? This approach could get confusing for you—particularly if you're a manager or are working on several projects with many team members. That's OK, and maybe it won't work for you because you need to follow company-wide standards. That doesn't mean you shouldn't take a personal approach. Think about it: if you put the time and effort into getting to know your team and creating a plan with them, everyone will buy in. In effect, they will communicate in a way that makes them comfortable and will deliver on your projects with less effort, confusion, and fear.

Inevitably, there will be times in any project where left-field ideas arise, new requirements surface, and questions occur that will come to you. Proceed with caution, project manager! If a client, partner, or team member is approaching you about any of these things, it's best to make sure the ideas check against your project scope, requirements, plan, and capabilities. The documentation isn't always the bottom line, but it's best to be open about any idea or conversation.

Knowing when to involve the team to help the conversation and the decision-making process is critical. As humans, we want to please others and get answers quickly. But sometimes that is just not possible. The last thing you want to do is answer a question or make a decision on behalf of your team only to find out that you were wrong. For instance, if a client is asking something that is design- or development-specific, pull in the appropriate people. They can help answer the question and possibly even do it better than you. That's where things get tricky: don't think of yourself as "just the PM," but recognize that you are "just the PM." Not the PM, design director, and consultant. It's more about owning your role and being honest about your expertise.

Set Communication Expectations

A general rule in project work should be that there's no such thing as over-communication. You need to be very detailed and constant when it comes to things like ever-evolving project requirements and tight timelines. If a detail is missed or miscommunicated, goals can be derailed, and you'll lose time and budget, as well as cause frustration.

So how do you stay on top of it? As a team, come to an agreement on how and when you will communicate. At the beginning of a project, sit down to discuss your budget, scope, timeline, requirements, and any other factors that might play into kicking off a new project. This will help to ensure that everyone on the team is aware of all of the critical pieces of information relating to project formalities.

In that meeting, be sure to assign specific project roles and the explicit responsibility of making sure that communication is flowing and is being documented in well-written meeting notes. But don't always rely on one person for notes, but rather make it a shared responsibility outside of meetings. For instance, if you're in a hallway and something interesting or impactful comes up organically in a discussion, don't forget to document it. Taking three to five minutes to share potentially critical info with your team could save you time and money.

Using a project communication/management tool to hold all of that information will facilitate good communication and knowledge sharing. Knowing when and where communication should happen, and how it will be documented is half the battle in the war against poor project communications. For a more complete discussion, see Chapter 11, "Facilitation for PMs."

Be Open to Collaboration

The most successful project teams are ones that are comfortable with tight collaboration, and that requires making time to share ideas, discuss and debate them, and make decisions together. It's not easy, but it's well worth the effort. Projects become stronger through those interactions, because they can help you do the following:

- Articulate project goals.

- Set better expectations about those goals and how you'll meet them.

- Formulate a project process that works for everyone.

- Discuss task dependencies and how they'll be met (or not).

- Communicate risks and issues—and solve them.

- Understand one another's roles and your impact on the project.

- Build a strong bond as a team.

- Enjoy your work.

Many times, uncontrollable factors (hard deadlines, locations, working hours, and the like) will place inevitable constraints on how teams collaborate on their own or with clients. But opening up your process to ideas from other team members and clients can make for more open, fun communications, and you might end up with some great, new ideas.

Good collaboration happens through the general understanding that your team is open to discussion. When setting your communication expectations early on, agree to collaborative sessions and open dialogue. From there, set up a series of sessions where you can discuss, sketch, and debate ideas as a team. Be sure to have a goal (or agenda) for each session and record takeaways. It's always easy to schedule a session and come up with 500 amazing ideas, but remember that you have to agree on and commit to at least one.

From there, keep your collaboration going with shared to-do lists. You can track subtasks as a team and keep each other in the loop on progress and dependencies with the help of a trusted app. There are a ton of tools out there, so find one that your team agrees on.

Once you've got your list documented, make sure that you've clearly assigned responsibility for it and check in often. If you see that a team member is behind, be proactive and comment on that to-do list. The point of an open list is to make sure that you're all up-to-date on the status of work at all times. A list like this will foster real-time communication, whether that is through in-person discussion, instant messenger, in-app messages, or email. The idea is to work in the open and share progress to build team support. This is the type of activity that helps people build products faster.

> **NOTE DON'T FORGET TO TALK!**
>
> Work is busy. Project management tools like TeamGantt, Slack, Basecamp, Trello, and many others can make busy days a little easier, but they can also get in the way of—or even distort—simple, human interactions. Don't forget about the value of face-to-face conversations, or even phone calls, when you want to move things along quickly.

Quick, Simple Communication Tactics

Relationship building (and joke telling) aside, think about your project communications in terms of routines. As a PM, you want to be sure that you're facilitating the flow of information in a way that feels expected. Doing so helps your team share information more easily or ask for it when it's needed. Some basic ways to ensure there is a consistent flow of information are the following:

1. **Establish what "success" means.**

   When you kick off a project, you'll want to make sure that your team and stakeholders are aware of what's expected of them throughout the course of the project—and for you to understand what's expected of you from the team as well. What's most important is to get the details on the table and ask, "What does success look like for us and how might we fail on this project?" Being truly honest about what's going to make you all feel good about the project when it's over—from the administrative end of the project to the front-line project communications—will help you set expectations early on.

2. **Discuss deliverables.**

   It's easy to check boxes off on a plan and do that on time. But if you're not actively checking in on those deliverables and reviewing them as a team, you're missing a huge opportunity to collaborate as a team and build a stronger product. When you're building your plan, make sure that you're working in some time for team deliverable reviews. Sit down and discuss or critique your deliverables. This will generate more confidence in what you're building and will also hold team members accountable for project decisions throughout the course of the project, even if they're not responsible for those items at the time. Essentially, through short review and discussion, you're eliminating the risk that a current deliverable will have a negative impact on your scope later in the project. It's well worth your time.

3. **Conduct status meetings.**

   Status meetings (scrum, stand-ups—whatever you call them as a team) are necessary. Create a routine that will keep everyone informed about progress or blockers. Maybe you'll meet daily as a team, or maybe it will be weekly. You should be able to make that decision as a team to ensure a good flow of information. You'll want to do that with your stakeholders as well to ensure that they're seeing progress and know where they fit in the process.

4. **Ask questions.**

   Being a PM requires you to be inquisitive—you have to understand processes, people, and deliverables. Chances are, you'll work with someone who comes up with a new way of working or takes a new spin on a deliverable. That's great! Just make sure that you understand it—and that you can articulate the what, why, when, and how of that new thing. And never be afraid to ask questions. Your team will likely be happy to share information or resources about the work to help you understand it better. And in the end, it's a win-win situation for you and your team, because the more you understand the work, the easier it is for you to advocate for it with stakeholders, or plan for similar activities in future projects.

5. **Schedule working sessions.**

   Scheduling collaborative brainstorming or "whiteboarding" sessions gets project team members invested in project ideas before they become more concrete, and it helps deal with potential scope issues. Simply having a developer sit with a designer to talk through the level of effort an idea might require can be a lifesaver when it's discussed before it goes to a client.

6. **Be the cheerleader.**

   You may not be a peppy cheerleader by nature, but every project needs a leader who owns and supports the process. A good project manager will enforce the process and keep everyone on the team in sync. Juggling timelines, deadlines, and deliverables is key, but a project manager who also supports the process, the team, and the client, brings true value to a project. Be the one who says, "Wow, this is really nice. Good work." Celebrate the wins and encourage the team to do the same.

7. **Play devil's advocate.**

   This is a tricky one—particularly because no one likes to be questioned. So, proceed with caution! But if you see something that might not be in line with project goals, or reminds you of an offhand comment from a client, raise it. Maybe you'd say

Innovating Project Communications

by Elizabeth Harrin
Elizabeth Harrin is a project management expert and director of the Otobos Group, a project communications consultancy based in London, England. She also founded **GirlsGuideToPM.com**, *a great resource for all PMs.*

I worked on a large software rollout that was going to fundamentally change the way people did their jobs. There was a lot of communication around what was happening, and I produced a monthly project newsletter that was sent out to heads of departments to cascade to their teams. When I visited some of the 40 affected locations, I'd often see it printed out and put on the wall, which was excellent. Some teams went above and beyond that, with their own local change champions managing a display of relevant information on an entire notice board.

That was fine in the early days, but when it really came to the countdown to go live, we knew we needed more. The project sponsor and I discussed how best to engage everyone—predominantly because what we were asking them to do was difficult. Change is always hard, and we knew this one was going to be a lot to ask. However, the business case was solid, and we also knew that it was going to happen. The challenge was bringing people along with us and knowing that communication was going to be key to driving that level of engagement.

something like, "Did you think about X?" and explain why you're thinking it. At the end of the day, you must look out for the best interests of the project and your team. This type of behavior not only supports your team and your project, but also shows everyone involved that you are genuinely engaged and not just worried about the PM basics.

8. **Informal check-ins.**

Between deadlines, check in on the upcoming document or delivery and chat with the team about what each will entail. Are your deliverables changing based on previous work? Will that impact the scope and the timeline? Explain the benefits of check-ins and how their constructive, helpful feedback will make the end deliverable stronger. Remember when it comes to setting expectations, there is nothing wrong with repeating yourself as long as your repetition is meaningful and timed just right.

We decided that an in-person presentation would enable us to discuss the impact and answer questions directly from a wide group of stakeholders. We did some planning. We worked out the logistics. And we realized that it would take over two months to do the job properly. It wasn't practical for us to take that much time away from managing the project to focus solely on this communication strand.

So we made a video of what we would have told them if we had been face-to-face.

It took some creativity to make a video about launching new software interesting. We included short video interviews with key stakeholders in each area, explaining why the project was important to them and how they and their teams were supporting it. We included screenshots and photos, too.

The video was watched by people at all locations, and we had excellent feedback on it. It was a simple way to promote the project, reach a wide audience, and give people a consistent message without having to meet them individually. On the plus side, we probably reached more people than townhall-style meetings. On the negative side, I had to rely on phone calls, emails, and capturing queries via the intranet instead of hearing and responding to questions face-to-face in real time. There are payoffs and choices in every communication decision.

by Holly Davis
Holly is an Agile project manager and delivery lead at Deeson,
a digital agency based in London, England.

About a year into my role as a project manager at an agency, I was given one of the largest projects I'd ever worked on. It was a big budget project with a team of three developers and one UX designer working full time for six months. We were brought in to work closely with the client's in-house development team and provide UX and front-end services for a complete site rebuild.

There were challenges around ensuring that there was enough UX/design done ahead of sprints started, that dependencies between stories were explicit, and that there was enough work for three developers to work on.

I found it really rewarding working on a project with three people from the front-end engineering team, because it's a rarity that a project arises where they can work as a team together on the same project. It was great to see them working together as a team and pushing for best practice and web standards to get the best result for the project and our client.

However, there were points in the project where I found it difficult to challenge some of the decisions being made on the project. For instance, it was fairly regularly that the team was asking for a significant amount of time in the sprint for "refactoring." For me, and for many PMs, reworking code that has already been shipped is a bit of a red flag. Sure, it often makes for stronger code and will be easier to update in the future, but spending time and budget on something that clients do not directly see, or experience a benefit from, can be difficult to communicate.

There was also occasional pushback from the developers in terms of constraints they faced when implementing the design. Over time, this caused friction between the designer and the developers working on the project. At points, the implementation failed to match the client-approved designs, and the developers would just say "it doesn't work," or "we used another component to make it more consistent." It often felt like the designs were being compromised, and the designer on the project was not invited to review the work or even consult with the developers to resolve issues together.

One of the elements of the project that helped to resolve these ongoing issues with reviews was visualizing the workflow. We used a physical Kanban board to track story level progress, i.e., the subtasks were tracked in JIRA, and the story level progress was tracked on the Kanban board.

We used different color cards for different team members and added a column for "design review." This was a really easy way to start embedding design reviews into our process. At first, it was difficult to get buy-in for the team to use the task board in addition to our online Kanban board. I suggested it in an end-of-sprint retrospective and said we would try it for one sprint to see if people found it useful. I invested time and energy in making it as engaging as possible, being creative and playful with the story titles and descriptions. By the end of the sprint, the team was actively using it to manage their workload, and everyone was keen to continue using it for the rest of the project.

The frequent end of sprint retrospectives gave the team feedback on what was going well and what wasn't. It also gave the team the opportunity to receive direct feedback from the client and helped us navigate through some of the more difficult interactions among team members.

With a long project like this, you may find that motivation trails off toward the end of the project. I certainly found that. This can be resolved to some extent by regularly changing the format of routine tasks or activities. Don't be afraid to vary and try new things. If it doesn't work, you don't need to do it again! I had great fun exploring different ways to run Scrum and different retrospective formats. And despite feeling reserved to begin with about how the client would respond, he loved it, too!

Body Language Speaks Volumes

You can do everything in your power to control your voice and tone, but your body can still manage to send a mixed message. In fact, a large part of communication and the way you're perceived comes from body language. Your deepest thoughts and feelings can be manifested through your facial expressions, eye movements, posture, stance, and gestures. That's a lot to think about on top of just getting the message right. Simple cues like keeping your arms uncrossed, smiling, not clenching your fists, and other things that you might just tend to do naturally will help you convey a more in-control and positive message. These actions can make you feel more self-confident and positive, which is evident to the people you're talking to. It's pretty powerful!

TL; DR

Successful project management starts with impeccable communication skills. There are a lot of factors that can make it difficult to master communications: processes, tools, and people. But you can do a better job communicating. Here are a few things to consider:

- Always be open and honest. There is no such thing as a project conversation or detail that you cannot share openly.

- Adapt your communication style to the project and people involved to get better results and build trust.

- Talk about the way you'll communicate and get everyone on board with some standard practices.

- Pick up the phone! Some of your best and most productive conversations will happen by phone or even (gasp!) in person.

- Find ways to get your team talking about the project. Set up sessions where you can collaborate and execute together. It will make you more productive and much happier as a team.

- Create communication routines to engage your team and keep expected communications going.

CHAPTER 8

Navigating the Dreaded Difficult Conversation

*Difficult conversations are a part of the job,
but also a part of life.*

I've always been a conscientious project manager-type, especially when I was a student. I never really disliked school or all of the work that came with it, but I was never really fond of group projects. And that's not because I didn't like my classmates; it was because I never felt 100 percent comfortable with everyone else's ability to get the work done in a cohesive way. Any time there was a group project, I would do everything I could to make sure that roles were clear, the work was defined, and the deadlines were set at least a few days in advance of our due date. See, I was a fully blossomed PM by college...lucky for my classmates, huh? (They likely wouldn't totally agree.)

The thing that made me get to that point was one chemistry project where I had to work with three other people to conduct an experiment, document it, and then present it in front of the class. Everyone outlined their pieces, we met to check in, and we discussed the work. As we got closer to the due date, it was becoming clear that one of my group mates was not pulling his weight. I wasn't the only one getting nervous—the two others on the team were as well. We didn't know what to do. We'd been checking in, and the deadline was looming, but he just didn't seem to care. The three of us discussed the matter one night. Should we do his work for him, just in case he didn't complete it? Should we tell the teacher? How would we make sure we got the grades we deserved without causing a major conflict and destroying a friendship at the same time?

In the end, we decided that we needed to address the issue with our teammate together. After all, it wouldn't be fair (or very mature) to "tell on him," and we knew that would just make matters worse. We sat him down and asked him what was going on. The conversation went something like this:

> **Us:** Hey, the project is due next week. Our parts are done, and we're waiting on yours to wrap up. We were hoping to have it done four days ago. What's up?
>
> **Him:** I'm working on it. Things have been really crazy for me lately. I'm sorry.
>
> **Us:** OK, well what can we do to get this done today? We're all very nervous and feel as though you're putting our good grades at risk. Not cool.
>
> **Him:** I said I was working on it.
>
> **Us:** We know, but we need to know when it will be done.

Him: My grandmother died. I have to go to her funeral tomorrow. I will work on it after that.

—SILENCE—

Us: Man, we are so sorry to hear that. And sorry for pressuring you. Let's work it out.

Him: Thanks. I will get it done, but I really just need the time.

Us: Yes, we totally understand. Maybe Professor Burk will give us an extension. We can prove to him how much of the work is done, and who wouldn't understand that you need some time? We'll handle it and let you know what happens. Focus on your family.

We had no idea that this could possibly be the outcome of the conversation. In fact, we expected it to be contentious. On one hand, I left the conversation feeling really awful for not thinking things through or asking about his work in another way. On the other hand, I was glad that we had talked to him and had a possible solution. The next day, the three of us went to Professor Burk's office to tell him what had happened. He gave us a one-week extension. We met the deadline and proudly got the grade we deserved. And all it took was 15 minutes of discussion to sort it all out.

I'm still friends with those three people today because that one conversation changed our friendship forever. We were able to be honest and vulnerable with one another, sort out a difficult situation, and succeed as a result.

The Anatomy of a Difficult Conversation

We've all been there. Someone did or said something you or someone on your team did not agree with, and you were the person who had to handle it. You actually didn't even want to handle it. Others knew that you didn't want to handle it. But if you're leading a team, it's part of your job description to keep the peace on your team—so you do what you can to make this conversation less awkward, edgy, tense, or even humiliating. But before you jump in, you'd better prepare, because these situations are never easy.

How do you assess a conversation to be sure you can handle it properly, especially when every individual perceives these exchanges differently? There is a lot that goes into any conversation—difficult or otherwise—but keep in mind that if you initiate the conversation, you'll want to think through every possible argument, statement, or outcome before you even speak a word about it. Your assessment won't always be correct, but dissecting the factors that will play into your conversation will help you understand the situation and the other person (or people) better—and conduct it like a professional.

The Situation

Every difficult conversation stems from an encounter, a situation, or a scenario. Think through it first. What actually happened and why? Chances are, you will hear multiple stories about a situation, but you will never know what truly happened without fully hearing all parties involved. Hearing a couple of accounts of the story might help you gain perspective, but it can also confuse or upset you. So this means that in many cases, you might have to stay neutral in order to get to an outcome that will work for everyone involved. The best way to stay neutral—because you must—is to listen and not provide any opinions or additional accounts of the story. Gather information, formulate your own opinions privately, and do what you can to simply understand what has happened.

If you are a part of the situation, but you want to resolve it with a conversation, it might mean that you have to remove your personal or emotional attachment to the issue and try to resolve it peacefully. A good way to do this is by figuring out how the outcome of the situation will affect the product/end user. Keeping things focused on the product and customer is a good way to rally the team back to a singular point of focus. This will certainly be difficult, and it will test your professionalism and workplace decorum, but you can do it. No matter what you do, keep in mind that we all have our own points of view, and we want to be heard. Give time and space for everyone to share their feelings about the situation, and the conversation will be less difficult.

> **NOTE** FACILITATING CONVERSATIONS
>
> *Six Thinking Hats* by Ed de Bono is a good resource for facilitating objective conversations, difficult or otherwise.

If it's helpful, jot down the issues you're seeing within the situation and break them down. For example, if the issue is that someone has missed a deadline, you might write these points down and use them as talking points later on:

- **The Issue:** You missed a deadline by three days.

- **The Impact:** Someone else on the team had to scramble to get their work done more quickly to make the final deadline. That person stayed late and came in early to get the work done. Upper management noticed it and is now questioning me about your reliability and accountability.

- **How I Feel:** Disappointed, worried. I also feel bad for the person who made up for your issue. You should thank them.

- **Resolutions:** You apologize to the person who made up time. We set up an internal schedule to review your work at least one day ahead of your deadlines.

Sometimes taking 5–10 minutes to think through your emotions and write them down can help you organize your thoughts—and possibly even find a resolution. Your personal example may be far more complicated than the previous situation, but if you think through the issue, impacts, feelings, and resolutions, you will prepare yourself for a productive outcome.

> **NOTE KEEP IT CONFIDENTIAL**
>
> Be careful about asking others about the situation. The last thing you want to do is create a back channel or gossip about it. Keep it to yourself and the other people involved, and you'll ensure trust and honesty.

The Other Person

There's always a culprit, and you'll have to handle that person, or people, with great care. Knowing the ins and outs of the situation before you approach this person about it is important, because you'll want some sense of how this person will approach the actual conversation. We all handle these conversations differently, so you really won't know how they'll react in advance.

Keep in mind that no one likes to be on the receiving end of a difficult conversation. You'll have to think about how to lighten the blow and to truly understand the situation to make it feel less difficult. Why did he or she do it? What's motivating him or her? And, are you worried about your relationship? Will this conversation be the way you'll interact from here on out? It could end up that way if you don't handle the situation with care.

The bottom line is that you must approach this conversation with a level of empathy if you want to truly resolve it and uphold the relationship.

You (and Your Emotional State)

You're probably scared. Or nervous. Or possibly even angry. It's totally normal. No one likes to call someone out. In fact, you might be frustrated or annoyed that you even have to address the situation. Wouldn't it just be easier to let it slide?

No, absolutely not. Letting one difficult conversation slide will not only set a precedent for accepting poor behavior, but it will also prove you to be a coward. It's not going to be easy to sit in front of someone and call them out for wrongdoing—but maybe you won't handle it that way. You'll address the issue head-on and share your own concerns or feelings about it (without making it about you).

First, figure out what is stopping you. Is it the fear of hurting someone else, the fear of destroying a relationship, or the fear of perpetuating a misunderstanding? That's a whole lot of fear, and it's completely normal to feel that way. You're a human being, and if you care at all about others or how they perceive you, you will be scared to address an issue head-on. But you have to set that fear aside by preparing yourself for the conversation, stepping up, and facing your fear (and the other person, as well as the issue).

> **NOTE** THEY SEE HOW YOU'RE FEELING
>
> It's OK to let your feelings show...because other people might see them anyway. When you experience a strong emotion but try to conceal your feelings, you let out a quick involuntary expression of emotion, or a micro expression. These often happen so fast that it's tough to see them in real time, but they're uncontrollable and sometimes obvious. Keep that in mind!

The Outcomes

Before stepping into the conversation, you should think about what you're hoping to get out of the conversation. Are you looking for an apology? A physical action to resolve the issue? Another meeting? Understanding exactly what you want from the situation will definitely help you formulate an approach for the conversation—and hopefully ease your fear.

Also, remember to think about how you will follow up on the outcome. There is nothing worse than talking through an issue, coming to a mutual agreement, and dropping it. Very often, it's the case that an issue won't be fully resolved with just one conversation. If you truly own the issue—and its healthy resolution—you will commit yourself to following up on it regardless of how uncomfortable that may be. So think through your ultimate outcome and a useful plan for how it can be rolled out. Maybe it will truly be one conversation. Maybe it will be a series of check-ins to discuss progress and feelings. Whatever you do, make it comfortable for everyone involved.

NOTE THERE IS ALWAYS A NEXT STEP

Talk about the plan. A simple, "Do you feel good about our next steps?" can go a long way toward solving an issue.

The Conversation

After you've taken some time to think about the situation, you'll be ready to approach the conversation. Put your fears aside and don't worry about being wrong. Remember, keep the other person's feelings in mind, and handle it in a way that feels positive and productive.

The best way to conduct a difficult conversation is in an open, honest way. You'll want to create a meeting atmosphere that promotes positive energy. Do whatever you can *not* to hold the meeting in your office or in a conference room. Go out for lunch or coffee instead— stay in a setting that feels neutral and less daunting. The pressures of work can seep into situations like this, and you want everyone's full attention, so go off-site and speak freely.

Don't Sweat It

Remember that you are at the heart of the anatomy of your difficult conversation. You can control the tone of the conversation if you approach the situation with the level of care it deserves. You'll obviously never be able to control what the other person contributes to the conversation, but you can be calm, understanding, and resolute with a little bit of preparation.

Are you feeling prepared to conduct a difficult conversation? The next section will highlight ways to handle the actual conversation with a level of comfort you never knew you could bring to the table.

Forcing a smile can actually make you happy. It sounds corny, but it's true: studies have found that if you change your facial expression to reflect a certain emotion, you may actually feel that emotion. Try it!

How to Conduct a Difficult Conversation

It's a fact: addressing situations that result in disagreement or tension can be stressful. No one wants to handle them, but sometimes you're put in positions where you just have to. Actually, these conversations do not have to be that difficult if you prepare yourself for a positive outcome.

Prepare Yourself

It's important to know what you are getting into when you address "difficult" conversations. While you don't want to script your conversation and get your mind set on one outcome, you do want to have an idea of how you will handle the conversation, and the possible outcomes—both positive and negative. Read "The Anatomy of a Difficult Conversation" to gather tips for preparing yourself for the best, and remember, it's your job to keep a healthy, positive attitude while trying to address the issue. It's easy to get worked up and upset, but at the end of the day, that will only stress you out more and show the other parties involved that you're not equipped to stay cool.

As soon as you've done your prep, you will be champing at the bit to just get the conversation over with. Maybe that's because you're eager to resolve it, or maybe it's because the stress of the situation is eating away at you, or maybe it's because the situation is getting worse. No matter the case, you won't want to spend too much time planning. Get to it and resolve the issue.

Impromptu Conversation

There's something nice about approaching someone briefly and just saying, "Do you have a few minutes to chat?" In general, it feels very nonconfrontational and in some ways it minimizes the magnitude of the situation. Use your judgment, but if you're trying to resolve an issue quickly and you think you'll be able to "grab" someone for a quick chat, do it.

Before you do, make sure that the other person is the type to be OK with being approached like this. Remember, a lot of people live and die by their calendars. An impromptu meeting could throw them off and upset them.

Scheduled Meeting

There is no doubt that scheduling a meeting will send a message. Many organizations require an agenda for any meeting scheduled—and many people will want to know what the meeting is about anyway. Be sure to think this through: will the person or people you're going to meet with react negatively if they know you're addressing the situation? Depending on the person or the situation, extra time to mull over the issue could make it even worse.

No matter what, the best path is to be 100 percent honest about the intent of the meeting. Keep a positive tone and express that the intent of the meeting is to discuss an issue and resolve it—together. The language you use and how you position the meeting will most definitely impact the mental state or attitudes that people will go into the meeting with.

Not sure how to handle it? Here are some traits or questions to consider when thinking through the venue for the meeting:

- What is the level of intensity of the situation? If it's one that could cause someone to be fired or quit, you will most likely want to call an immediate, impromptu meeting.

- How well do you know the person or people? Personalities play a large role in how you handle these interpersonal situations. If you know the person and feel a more relaxed approach will work, call an impromptu meeting.

- What's your workplace culture? If you call an impromptu meeting, can you run out together for coffee or lunch? Or will you have to stay in the office? Where the meeting takes place can certainly impact how people feel about it. Keep in mind, while a formal atmosphere may feel necessary for more serious situations, a relaxed atmosphere—like a coffee shop—may be more conducive to conversation and working issues out in a relaxed, friendly way.

You will need to pick an approach, time, and format that you feel will work best for the situation and the people involved. Sometimes, you'll get it right; other times, you may not. No matter how you handle it, admit mistakes and stick to your decisions and work hard to resolve the issue.

Meeting Means Talking *and* Listening

As soon as you've pulled everyone together—whether it's a one-on-one or group meeting—establish the purpose of the meeting. You are together to resolve the issue. In order to get there, express the desire to have everyone be happy and heard, not just to avoid interpersonal issues or conflict, but for the health of your work. These meetings can bring on a level of stress that makes people uncomfortable, so they often do not realize that their personal opinions and emotions can get in the way of a productive outcome. When they do get in the way, work and working relationships fail. Be sure to express a goal that everyone can agree on: to speak freely and be heard.

Start with a general description of the issue. Keep it high level and don't add color commentary to the story. State the facts and follow them up with ground rules for your meeting:

1. **The purpose of the meeting is to resolve the issue at hand.**

   Issue management can be confusing. People will have varying opinions on any given scenario, and it's your job to listen to all of them. Facts will be hard to check or verify, and you'll sometimes feel like you're caught in a web of disaster. But you can stand in the middle and ensure that everyone is heard and that each story, point, or argument points to a resolution.

   First, end the issue right then and there. Turn the focus from finger pointing to resolving. You want the team to know that the issue has ended and that you're in this meeting to end it together. Additional finger pointing or arguing will only make the issue worse and drag out the outcome you want and need.

2. **Speak now or forever hold your peace.**

    The environment of this meeting is one of discussion. In order to keep a positive attitude about a resolution, everyone should have a chance to be heard. Do your best to moderate the meeting and make sure that all parties have a chance to speak up. This may mean that you go around the room and have everyone state how they feel about the issue. Or maybe you will bring in an outside moderator to ensure that all parties are being vocal. (They could do the job of calling on people and asking them how they feel.)

    However you handle it, be sure to consider all parties and where they sit in the situation. Some people will be heated and will speak up. Others will be quiet and listen. Try to maintain a balance and allow everyone to weigh in, but don't cut anyone off. When you close the meeting, be sure that everyone has said their piece. If they haven't, you'll open the door for additional issues—or resentment—to creep in.

3. **Listen.**

    Establish a modicum of respect. Everyone will not only have a chance to speak, but everyone will also be expected to listen. This means not cutting people off, no side conversations, and no questions unanswered.

    Again, you might want someone to moderate this conversation if you've got a larger group. If that's not possible, do your best to keep the flow of conversation headed in the direction of an out-come. Don't let one person dominate the conversation and don't let an issue go unaddressed. Conversations can wind around ten different ways with one comment. If you feel as though things are getting off track, keep notes or track issues mentioned on a whiteboard that everyone can see. This will ensure that everyone is not only given a chance to speak, but also that their issues—large or small—are being heard.

4. **The meeting will not end without a resolution—or a plan for one—in place.**

    If you truly want to address the issue, you must come up with a resolution for it. This is the point of your meeting, of course. Moreover, you want to come to an agreement of that solution as a team. As you circle the issues through conversation, ask "How can we resolve it?" of the attendees. Or suggest solutions as you see fit.

Letting attendees know that this meeting is not just a venue to complain, but one to resolve the issue at hand—together—will greatly impact the way your conversation happens. This is especially true if your meeting is taking place with limited time. Possibly think of a rough agenda for the discussion. It could look something like this:

1. Identify issue.

2. Discuss outcomes.

3. Team decides on a solution or action plan.

4. Discuss next steps.

Keeping focus on the outcome will keep you on track. If you give the group a goal, they will focus on the solution more than the problem.

Avoid Verbal Conflict

Heated conversations or situations tend to bring out the worst in people. Whether that means taking over a conversation, raising voices, cutting others off, or simply re-stating ideas as their own. There are a lot of things that people can do—intentionally or unintentionally—to make others more angry or upset. So when you step into a forum that feels heated, keep yourself in check. You never want to be seen as the person who can't keep their cool.

That said, there is nothing worse than being cut off—or flat out ignored—when you're trying to make a point. Check out these quick tips to make sure that you can stand your ground on the meeting or debate battlefield:

- **Set expectations with the room at the top of the meeting.** Simply say, "I know this conversation is a big one, and we all have things to say. Let's please show each other respect and not step on each others' toes. We'll all have time to make our points." This will hopefully put some people on notice and allow others to get a word in.

- **Set expectations again when you're about to make your point (particularly if it's a long one).** Start off by saying, "I have a few things to say, so please give me the time to make my point. I am more than open to your ideas, but I just want to be sure I can state my thoughts in full."

- **If you're really intent on making a point, keep talking.**
  Sometimes someone needs to be talked over to understand that
  what they are doing is rude. Or maybe you'll stop briefly and say,
  "Sorry, I am not done. Let me finish." You'll know what works
  when you're in the moment—you just can't be bashful.

- **Let's say you let that person talk over you.** Hear them out.
  Understand what they are saying and use that information to
  ask them questions, or even make or strengthen your own point.
  When you are polite and it shows, you win, no matter what. Why
  is that? People will be more inclined to work with you, listen to
  you, and show you the respect you deserve. Meeting room bul-
  lies never get that respect.

- **Be ready to give in.** Sometimes these arguments are not worth
  battling over. You can always follow up with someone separately
  to express your concerns or share more ideas in full. True professionals can sense when the time and place are right, so use that
  instinct here.

NOTE CROSSED ARMS? BE CAREFUL!

Keep your body language in mind during this meeting, and think
about the people you're speaking to. Body language can be
interpreted differently by a variety of cultures, and the last thing
you want to do is upset someone!

Use Thoughtful Language

The way you express your emotions, describe facts, and even
interact with others in this meeting will impact the course of the
conversation. Disagreements are tricky because they might be about
a hard, cold fact, but emotions always come into play. As humans,
we express our feelings in different ways. One person might show
outright anger through harsh language, while another might be calm
and collected but express the same ire. Either way, be mindful of
your language and how it could be perceived.

Inclusive language shows the team that you are invested in resolving the issue with them, not for them. It also shows that you are
dedicated to rebuilding the trust of the team and strengthening the
bond of the working relationship. No matter how it ends, you want to
share a common feeling of respect and dignity, and that can be done
with using words that are:

- **Inclusive of everyone:** We, us, our, team

- **Polite:** Please, thank you, excuse me

- **Solution oriented:** Next steps, solution/resolution, plan

> **NOTE** EMOTIONS ARE CONTAGIOUS!
>
> Research has proven that people unconsciously mimic the emotional expressions of those around them. Keep that in mind when you're around your team. If you're miserable, they might catch on—or a simple smile could make their day better.

Finding the Right Solution

Discussing (or complaining about) issues is easy. Finding solutions that work for everyone can be difficult. Guide the conversation in a way that points all parties to possible solutions. Here are some scenarios and quick solutions that could help you.

Personal Conflict

It happens: two people have a professional disagreement, and it escalates. Maybe you're one of those people. If you are, address the issue head-on. Approach the person and talk to them about a way to fix it together. If you're managing people who are in conflict, it might be best to have them sort it out on their own. The best thing to do is ask them to speak to one another before involving you. Facilitating a solution can be far more successful than prescribing one.

Group Conflict

If an issue is impacting a larger group, you'll have to conduct a meeting. After everyone has had a chance to speak, transition the meeting to solutions. You might not hear solutions, so it could be up to you to identify them for the group.

Of course, there will be times when no one likes any of the solutions raised. That's fun! If it does happen, ask for alternatives and discuss why the solutions proposed will not work. If you run out of time, start a collaborative document and follow up within 24 hours to see what you have come up with.

There's a definite chance that you'll end up frustrated in group situations, because it's hard to gain consensus. At some point, you will need to be the authority figure and decide on an outcome. This can be unnerving, because the decision sits only with you, and you become acutely aware of how the success or failure of the solution will be seen as yours and yours alone. If you're working with a team, you don't want to operate that way. Do your best to share the burden of the decision and involve individuals in the execution of the plan. This will spread that feeling of accountability.

Follow-up

Whether your issue is big or small, with one person or tens of people, you need to follow up on your solution to ensure that it's actually working. This can be done with one-on-one meetings to help you understand and monitor progress and feelings. Make sure that your plans are clear and that your communications about them support it 100 percent. This can also be done with in-person meetings or even simple team status updates via email or in a shared communication tool. Do whatever feels right for your team and do everything you can to pay attention to the details and rebuild (or help rebuild) trust and relationships.

The Most Difficult Conversation I've Ever Taken On

Years ago, I was working at a large agency on high-profile projects with major corporate clients. This made for an intense project setting with many moving parts, people, and deadlines. It was critical for the team to be working like a well-oiled machine, and it was my job to keep it that way. But, of course, I couldn't.

We were one month from a site launch, and the clients were still going back and forth on color decisions—a simple change that could impact all of our work. It was frustrating for everyone, but I was trying to keep the team's spirits up. But there was one person who just couldn't muster the energy to have a positive attitude: the designer.

I got it. In fact, *I got her*. Not only was this a frustrating situation that was difficult her not to take personally, but she also had a personality that gravitated toward negativity. She was sarcastic and quiet—quali-ties that many, many people can take the wrong way, particularly in a stressful work setting. And they did. I got a handful of desk visits and instant messages all about the designer's attitude. It was enough that I knew I needed to address it quickly, or it would damage team morale. So I initiated the difficult conversation that afternoon.

I stopped by the designer's desk and asked if she had a few minutes to talk. We took a short walk and got a cup of coffee around the corner from the office. I wasn't sure how to start the conversation. It was awkward because I kind of knew what her response would be. But I prepared myself for the worst (remember that college story I told earlier). I jumped right in:

Me: Hey, I just wanted to talk for a few minutes because there's an issue I am seeing with the team that I wanted to let you in on.

(I didn't want to point the finger right away because that would open things up in a very negative way.)

Her: Yeah, what's that?

(Not happy. I was not surprised.)

Me: Well, we are *this close* to launching the project, and I know it has been a challenge for everyone, you in particular.

(Expressing some empathy here.)

But I'm worried about how you're feeling about it, and so are others. Is the project dragging you down?

Her: What? No. That's just who I am. You know me by now. I'm not a smiley, happy person, and when I am constantly dealing with bullshit client requests, I don't get happier.

(Again, no surprise here. A huge sigh within.)

Me: Right. Well, the thing is that you're worrying the team and bringing them down. I know you probably don't mean to, but it's happening. A couple people have raised concerns.

Her: Why not just come to me?

(I knew this was coming too! This was my chance...)

Me: Well, I think they felt comfortable talking to me about it because they see it as more of a project risk, and they don't want to burden you any further. They know you are stressed, but they also don't feel comfortable with the way you are handling it.

(That was fair, not candy-coated.)

That's why I decided to talk to you today so we could just handle it. Is that fair?

Her: Sure. I mean, I don't want to upset anyone. I never really thought I would bring anyone else down. I feel kind of bad.

Me: Don't feel bad! You're under a lot of pressure, and we all know it. But let's figure out some ways that you can maybe channel that negative energy and not let it get to the team. I mean, you can vent to me as much as you need/want, you know that, right?

Her: Yeah, thanks. I'm going to think about this some more. Thanks for bringing it to me in this way, though. I appreciate it.

That was that. She thought about it and followed up with me. The outward complaining to the team stopped and the venting instant messages to me started. I didn't mind that, because I understood. And I knew I could help her make light of the negative situation. As a PM, I wished that I had someone I could reach out to in the same way! Eventually, I did. It was my new designer friend.

Say Hello to Agreement and Goodbye to Disagreement

When you've made it through the prep, the meeting, and ended up with a workable solution, you'll feel gratified in knowing that you played a key role in fixing the issue. But there is one thing to be said: conducting a difficult conversation never gets totally easy. And we all know that disagreements pop up now and again, so you'll be tasked with sorting out a new issue at some point. Using the tactics presented in this chapter, you'll be able to assess a situation, put your emotions aside, and plan for a positive outcome.

TL; DR

Face it: no one likes a difficult conversation. But if you're managing people, you will have to face them head-on. Follow this advice to ensure that you're handling them well:

- Be sure to understand the issue first and set your personal feelings aside.

- Have empathy for the people involved and do what you can to understand their points of view.

- Think through the outcomes of the conversation before conducting it.

- Respect privacy and preserve the personal relationships.

- Use thoughtful language.

- Have a follow-up plan for your meeting.

CHAPTER 9

Setting and Managing Expectations

Don't let others set expectations for you.

When I was a kid, my parents took me to Disney World. Leading up to the trip, all I could think about was meeting Mickey Mouse—at his house, one-on-one. I was five, so I had no idea what Mickey's house looked like, but I knew I'd find it, and we'd sit down and talk. I was wrong. Not only was there no house, I wasn't going to get my one-on-one time with my idol. In fact, I'd have to shove my way through a bunch of other kids to get in front of him. I barely got a minute with him, but I got a hug. Still, I was crushed.

· · ·

Thinking back, I realize that I was pretty much set up for disappointment. I remember specifically saying I could not wait to meet Mickey and see his house. I probably said it about 75 times leading up to the trip. My parents laughed it off and carried on. After all, I was five, and they thought the notion of me meeting Mickey was cute. What they didn't think to do was tell me that my dreams were grandiose. Had they informed me of how it likely would have worked out, I wouldn't have been so upset.

This was my first lesson on managing expectations—or rather missing expectations and knowing how it feels to be on the other side of the fence. Had my parents made one simple statement, my outlook on that day and my feelings and behaviors would have changed.

Fast forward 30+ years—I'm on a project, and I'm seeing the same thing happen all over again. We had a wonderful project kick-off meeting where we did some collaborative brainstorming. Great ideas were sketched and discussed. We took them back to the office for project inspiration, knowing that not every idea would be used. When we presented our first round of ideas, our clients asked, "What about that cool home page feature we sketched at the kick-off?" Oh, right, that. Well, we decided that didn't work with the rest of the site design, so we opted for a different feature. We can't design them all.

But why didn't we just *say* that in the kick-off meeting? If we were really doing our jobs, we would have set the simple expectation of what would actually come out of those collaborative sessions. Idea generating, team building, and eventually a prioritization of what could be included based on research, design aesthetic, scope, and timeline. Just like the Disney World situation, one simple statement would have set the tone for what to expect out of that one meeting. Lesson learned.

We All Have Expectations

Our most successful projects are established with clearly defined goals. From day one, we can embark on a project journey and know what we're striving for. How we get there can be a whole different story, but if you're managing projects (and personalities) you should do your best to make the actual journey as crystal clear as those goals. If you truly want to make that journey easy, you'll work hard to set and manage the expectations of your team, clients, stakeholders, and anyone else who may be taking part in or watching your project from the sidelines. If you don't set and manage expectations from day one, you're going to be in for a miserable ride. Get ready for missed deadlines, hemorrhaging budgets, and tons of difficult conversations with very unhappy people.

Set Expectations Before the Project Begins

The best way to set expectations is early and often. As a project manager who sits between an internal team and a client, you have to be very detailed and persistent when it comes to communications and relaying vital parameters to the collective team for what to expect at every turn of a project. If you're not laser focused on the details, things like project requirements and tight timelines will become painful issues for everyone to deal with. If a detail is missed or miscommunicated, goals can be derailed, time can be vaporized, budgets compromised, and frustration catalyzed. And the PM will always—always—be blamed for it.

So how do you stay on top of it? From day one on a project, be very clear about what should be expected of you as the PM, your team, your process, and your clients. Every person and aspect is integral to the success of the project, and it's better to lay it all out; loopholes all too often set the stage for scope creep, confusion, and conflict to manifest.

Understand Your Scope

Chances are, if you're a project manager, projects are sold or initiated and then assigned to you to lead. In an agency setting, you're suddenly armed with a scope of work (SOW), a team, and a phone number for your new client. If you're managing an internal team, you're given a brief, a deadline, a team, and maybe some requirements. Either way, starting a new project can be really daunting, and it's up to you to figure out just how you will get it done. But before you even think about planning, you'd better sit down and read every page of that SOW or project brief and take notes. You'd be surprised by how little details can creep into a document like this, so review it in depth to make sure that you do not have any questions. Specifically, be sure you're looking for the following information:

- Goals of the project

- Budget for the project

- Deadline for the project (and the compelling reasons to meet that deadline)

- Requirements for what is to be built, including:

  - Design or branding elements to be used

  - A specific technology that will require certain expertise

  - A list of required functionality to be designed/built

  - Outside factors to be considered, such as external systems, APIs, and even partners or agencies

- People who will be involved, including:

  - Client team (what are their roles, and who are your decision makers?)

  - Stakeholder groups involved (management, executives, boards)

  - Partners (third party agencies, developers, designers, etc.)

- Special project requirements, including:

  - Terms for billing that the project timeline must adhere to

  - Milestone or delivery review processes

  - Clauses on timeline delays

  - Requirements for specific meetings

After you've done your due diligence, request a meeting with the person or people who can answer all of your questions. This may be a sales person, a manager, a project manager, or even a project stakeholder. The beginning of your project is just as critical as the launch or delivery of it, so make sure you treat it that way; don't let any minor question go. The more you know about the project and its background or intent, the more confident you will be in leading a team to manage it. Plus, just showing that you're fully invested in the project early on will exhibit your true position as the project leader.

THE SALES CONUNDRUM

Many agency PMs find themselves handed projects with budgets that don't match the effort. The only way you can overcome this issue and get projects with adequate budgets is to change your sales process. Find a way to have your sales conversations documented and shared with your project teams. Work together to create project estimates in the sales process and start projects on the right foot.

KEEP THAT SOW HANDY

Your project contract is something you need to know inside and out. Be sure to keep a copy of it on hand. You may even want to print it out and makes notes on it. Whatever you do, make sure that you can pull it up when you're on a call or in a meeting because whenever it's in question, everyone will look to you for answers.

Pre-Kick-off Meetings

Once you're 100 percent comfortable with your scope, get ready to talk about it with everyone who will have a role in executing it. At the beginning of a project, set up two separate meetings—one with your team and one with your stakeholders—to discuss all of the detailed documents and processes that will make or break your project. Things like scope, timeline, requirements, and even reviews of conversations that were conducted during the sales process can be very valuable to anyone who is invested in a new project. Review the formal documents using a low-pressure discussion—even a Q&A—to make those things feel more accessible and understandable. This will help to ensure that everyone on the team has had a chance to get their questions or issues addressed, and that they are aware of all of the critical pieces of information relating to the project.

Sample Client Pre-Kick-off Meeting Agenda

- **Introductions:** Kick it off by telling your new client how excited you are to work on their project. Be genuine—talk about the features, subject matter, or whatever else seems like a good fit for your team. Then introduce the team. Talk about their expertise, project interests, and what they will be responsible for. You can set the right tone for your project with this meeting, so make it equal parts comfortable and informative.

- **Review scope:** As it turns out, your client may not have read the final version of your SOW. So review it at a high level. You don't have to read it line by line, but at least call out the main points. Are there goals, terms, or specific deliverables to review? If yes, then talk about them now before they can become questions or issues. At the end of this meeting, you want to be sure your client understands what is included and excluded in your scope of work.

- **Discuss the timeline:** The biggest expectation on a project can be the deadline, so talk about it. Be clear about the final delivery date and ask what's driving that date. Is there an event or campaign tied to the launch of your project? You'll want to know about those things now so that you can set the right expectation for how you will make that date. Discuss reviews and approvals of your deliverables and make it very clear what potential dependencies will be. Also, be sure to bring up delays, because they always happen! But if you discuss how you will handle those potential project delays now, you will set the right expectation for timing.

- **Discuss project requirements:** Every project comes with requirements, whether they are tied to look and feel, functionality, or even content. You need to be sure that you have these things documented. If detailed project requirements already exist, review them and make sure that you completely understand what is expected of the project based on what they indicate. If they aren't documented, start the conversation and talk about how you will come to an agreement on what's needed. (We'll get into the specifics for how to document requirements later in this chapter.)

- **Discuss project communications:** Your project will fail if you're not in agreement on how you will communicate through the course of the project. Will you use a communication tool to document conversations, or are you OK with email? Will you schedule a regular call to discuss updates and progress? Do what will help you set the proper expectation of what's happening and what's to come on your project. Invariably, what works with one person may not be a good fit for another. So you'll need to adjust your approach based on the discussion you have in this meeting. Come to the meeting with suggestions for what works for your team, and don't leave the meeting without agreement on the avenues and frequency of communications.

- **Next steps:** It's always helpful to recap expectations and assignments. Help keep your team and clients on target by reminding them of what's next on their plate. Take a few minutes to call out action items and next deliverables before ending any meeting. And always follow up with meeting notes!

Assign Project Roles with a RACI Matrix

Large projects can be complex: tasks often overlap, are dependent on other tasks, or are so voluminous in scope that more than one team member ends up working on them. If you don't set expectations on who does what and when, staffing and responsibilities can get confusing quickly. Be sure to assign specific project roles and the explicit responsibility for each task, as well as making sure that communication is flowing according to agreed-upon standards. A helpful tool in determining team responsibilities is a RACI matrix (see Table 9.1), which describes the way that various roles participate in completing tasks or deliverables for a project or business process. It is especially useful in clarifying roles and responsibilities in cross-functional/departmental projects and processes. The acronym RACI represents: responsible, accountable, consulted, and informed.

TABLE 9.1 SAMPLE RACI MATRIX

Task	Project Manager	Content Strategist	UX Designer	Graphic Designer	Front-End Developer	Back-End Developer
Project Plan	R, A	C, I	C, I	C, I	C	C
Site Map	A	C	R	I	I	I
Wireframes	A	C	R	C	I	I
Homepage Design	A	C	C	R	C	I
CMS Setup	A	I	I	I	C	R

Roles of the RACI

Rather than thinking about the roles of your team by practice area or even title, think about them in terms of who is responsible for what. For instance, if you have two UX designers on a project and 10 UX tasks, you'll want to make clear who is responsible for what. That will help you to avoid double work, dwindling budgets, and disappointed team members. Below is a list of each RACI role and a definition for each.

- **Responsible:** The team member who does the work to complete the task. There will be at least one person on your team who is the responsible party, sometimes more.

- **Accountable:** This is the person who delegates work and is the last person to review the task or deliverable before it is deemed complete. There must be only one accountable specified for each task or deliverable. *Note:* It may not be your PM! Also, you may find that the responsible party is also the accountable one.

- **Consulted:** Every deliverable is strengthened by review and consultation from more than one team member. Consulted parties are typically the people who can provide input based on how it may affect their work later on the project or have some domain expertise on the deliverable itself.

- **Informed:** Some team members don't need to work on every deliverable, but it's best to keep them in the loop on project progress.

NOTE ADAPT TO YOUR USE

The RACI is a pretty formal way of figuring out who will do what. It may feel too formal for you, especially if you are on a small team. If that's the case, that is OK! Just remember to always keep a clear definition of responsibilities as they relate to project tasks, and you'll be A-OK.

Document Requirements

It would be nice to start every project with a set of marching orders or a laundry list of what's needed. The problem with that approach is that it leaves little room for creativity or innovation. Plus, when you build a list without actually discussing it, you'll likely miss or misinterpret something. That's why it's important to understand the people you're working with and their motivations. Yes, sometimes you have to play mind reader. Well, not completely! You've got to ask the right questions to get what you need. That means getting into their heads and figuring out what they want. It's definitely not easy.

Dig for Information

Before you plan or build anything, and as you begin to get to know your clients and their business, make time to identify the high-level business requirements of your project. This practice will ensure a clear understanding of what must be included in your project. You won't need to worry about getting too much in the weeds at first. Gather the high-level business requirements right away, and your detailed functionality requirements will follow.

> **NOTE** THINK LIKE A CLIENT
>
> It's important to remember that not all stakeholders think like you do in terms of features, functionality, and time to build. In fact, it could be a big black box for them. This is your chance to connect their business goals and requirements to your project.

The best way to understand what your stakeholders actually want is to ask questions. Shocker! Here's the thing: you can't necessarily take a cookie-cutter approach to every project. Sure, you may have some core questions to use (we'll get to those). But before you dump a set of questions on your stakeholders, be sure you understand what you are asking and why. It may be helpful to ask yourself these questions first:

1. What requirements information already exists in the SOW, project brief, or supporting documentation?

2. What kind of information am I looking for?

3. How will this information help the project and my team?

4. Is there any question about what can be done within the scope of this project?

5. Where is there confusion?

6. Do I understand my client's business and how our project goals map to it?

7. Will these requirements help me set the proper expectations?

8. Am I about to ask the *right* people these questions?

Answers = Documented Requirements

The answers to your questions will eventually turn into expected interactions, features, or functionalities that will help you begin your requirements documentation. So, set yourself up for future iterations of your requirements documentation by formatting these responses in a readable, shareable format. This will set the expectation of what goals the project will meet, and how what you will deliver will map back to those goals. The best way to document these requirements is in a spreadsheet or list that works for your team. Essentially, what you *must* document are the following:

- **Requirement name and number:** A unique name that describes what is being discussed and can be easily referred to. You'll want to number these in case you have many and can easily find them in your document.

- **Requirement description:** A simple statement that defines the business need the requirements fulfill.

- **Category:** A group identifier for similar requirements that all project resources will understand. This could be the section in your site map, a technology, etc.

- **Notes:** A place to capture questions (yours or the client's) that will surface as a requirement evolves.

As soon as you've documented the high-level business requirements, you're ready to compile the questions you need to ask to get into the true details. Start broad with a top-level question about functionality and use the response to dig deeper. Here's an example question with follow-up questions that could arise:

"Will your site require users to log in?"

> Does registration require payment?
>
> Will the site display a logged-in user's name?
>
> > *First and last name, or username?*
>
> Where is login information stored currently?
>
> > *Will it stay there?*
>
> Do logged-in users have access to more information or functionality than non-logged-in users?
>
> What happens if a user forgets his or her password?
>
> Do you have error states currently designed into your system?

There are several questions that could come out of one single response, and each response could add requirements to your work. That means that one simple "yes" or "no" answer could have a cost attached to it. So this exercise is important to understand what your team can do within your scope.

Teamwork

Gathering requirements is something that your whole team should be responsible for, because one simple requirement could have different timeline and scope impacts for each resource. For instance, a Twitter feed might take a designer 20 minutes to design, while a developer might need a few hours to find and execute the right solution.

As soon as you've determined all answers related to a piece of functionality, add them to your requirements document. An example might look like Table 9.2.

TABLE 9.2 SAMPLE REQUIREMENTS DOCUMENT

Requirement ID	Requirement Name	Description	Category	Notes
1.0	Login	Users must be able to register or log in from all pages	Header	
1.1	Login, payment	Registration payment	Header	When a user clicks on register, she will be directed to reg form with payment options: Visa, MC, AMEX, PayPal

You may be adding to this document through the course of your design phase—and that's OK, as long as you are sharing these new requirements with your team and having an open conversation about how they might impact your budget or timeline. This is the ultimate tool in setting project expectations because there might come a point where you've added too much to this list and you've got to prioritize features. If you've got all the items in a spreadsheet, you can rate each item in terms of effort and decide what's in and what's out. Finally, when it's time to launch your project, this document can serve as your final checklist to make sure you've delivered as promised.

Manage Expectations

As soon as you've laid the foundation for what to expect on the project, it's your job to maintain those expectations and manage them as new ideas, issues, and details arise. On any healthy project, expectations can change over time. It's your job to continue the conversation about those expectations and ensure that they're not being missed at any point in your process. It can take as little as 30 minutes a week to keep your project in check, so make the time and keep things running smoothly with some simple techniques.

Foster Good Communications

You've got to be a good communicator and facilitator in order to lead a team and set and manage the right expectations for everyone involved. At the same time, you've got to help others communicate and foster openness on your project. If you've done your job, your team will understand that over-communication is welcomed, because the more you know about their progress or potential issues, the more you will be able to help them resolve issues. With open communication, your team will always know what is happening, will set their own expectations, and will likely meet timeline and budget expectations without question. If your clients' expectations are outlined and discussed, they'll be happy that they've helped you meet or exceed them, and will be reassured because they most likely know what to expect from the final product.

Build a Communications Plan

If you're managing a large project with a lot of stakeholders, you should consider building a communications plan. This kind of documentation will ensure that everyone involved in your project is fully clear on who is working on the project, how you will work together, and how you will document and communicate issues, status, and special circumstances. Essentially, a good plan will ensure that you have effective communications throughout the life of your project. It takes some effort to pull together, but it can be invaluable if you're in need of some guiding principles for your project.

A basic communications plan should include the following information:

- **Plan's purpose and approach:** A high-level statement of why the plan exists and why it's important to follow.

- **Communication goals and objectives:** A list of reasons why/ when your teams will need to communicate in order to keep your project on track. Examples of this could be:

  - Project status updates on tasks, timelines, and budget

  - Deliverable presentations and feedback sessions with key stakeholders

  - General project presentations to larger audiences (e.g., board of trustees, executive management, etc.)

- **Communication roles:** Your whole team will have a role in communicating and so will your clients. Define who is the key point of contact, as well as the additional team members who will play a role in the project at certain points.

- **Communication tools and methods:** Define the tools you have agreed to use and how you will use them. This is a great place to define the routine communications you'll create, like status reports.

- **High-level project communication messages:** Outline certain points or milestones in your project that will change the way you will communicate and who the communications will be directed to. This will ensure that your messages are seen by the right people. Depending on how large the organization is, you may want to map out a hierarchy of which people see communications and when, depending on the level of decision being made. This can get very tricky, so it's good to get it out in the open early on.

Your communication plan can take shape in several ways: it could be a formalized document, a page on your project intranet, a spreadsheet, or a nicely designed PDF. No matter what form it takes, make sure that it actually speaks to your clients and stakeholders. Take the time to review it in depth with them and make the details very clear. This document will set very clear expectations on how you will communicate and how you will be communicated to, so getting it right and approved early on is critical.

Conduct Status Meetings

One of the best ways to manage expectations is to discuss them on a regular basis. You can do that very easily by setting a routine that provides you with project information around progress, tasks, to-do lists, and blockers. Not only does sharing that information help a team work together and make everyone feel included, but it also helps to have a general understanding of what to expect on any given day on a project. Whether you're a one-man team or a team of 20, working in an office or remotely, sharing progress is one of the most important things you can do in order to keep communication flowing. A common and helpful way of doing this is by implementing project status meetings.

Team Status

In general, a 15-minute in-person (or via videoconference/phone) review of the day's tasks is a nice way to catch up with your team and can work to your advantage. There are several ways to conduct a status call, so be flexible and work with your team to determine what to do.

Simply go around the room and give everyone a chance to talk about what they're working on that day. A quick check-in will force everyone to organize project priorities prior to the meeting, adding to a feeling of accountability for tasks. Before wrapping things up, it's always helpful to ask, "Does anyone need help or have time to help with tasks if needed?" Doing so helps you build trust and rapport with your team.

How you approach status meetings will depend on the project you're working on, your team's schedules, and maybe even the intensity of the work. At some point in a project, you might feel like you need to check in a few times a day, maybe because you're handling lots of moving pieces, or you need to make sure that everyone is on track. Remember: communication is good!

Client Status

It's a good practice to keep an open, consistent line of communication with your clients. Ensure that you're staying current on all project issues by providing a weekly status report in the form of a written notification or phone call, and check in regarding alignment with project objectives.

Status reports not only help you and your clients stay on track, but they also help keep you honest about your work, process, budgets, and issues. Making the time to sit down and discuss these things pays off in terms of your relationship with the client and with helping your team see it through to completion. When you conduct regular status meetings, you're ensuring that the expectations you established in the beginning of your project are consistently reviewed and reaffirmed as you proceed to the delivery of the final product. These regular check-ins give you an opportunity to build the relationship, but also be sure to make time to talk about non-project related things. Find some common ground, like hobbies or interests, and make small talk. When you've built a relationship that is based on trust and friendship, it makes the more difficult news easier to swallow. Plus, you're a human—you have to find ways to connect with the people you're working with.

Reveal the Difficult News

Are you going to go over the budget on a project? From a client's perspective, there is nothing worse than finding out about a project issue that could have been avoided until it's too late. Use the status report and meeting as a way to communicate and discuss the issue. Pull that report together, hop on the phone, and keep an open dialogue going.

NOTE A GOOD STATUS REPORT

A good status report covers the following information:

- What was done last week?
- What is being done this week and next week?
- What are the action items?
- What is the update on the timeline?
- What is the update on the budget?
- What are the potential project risks?

Take and Share Notes

Expectations are rooted in conversations. The things people say in meetings, hallway conversations, and online chats can have a major impact on what you do on your project. So it's critical that you create a project culture of documenting conversations and sharing details with everyone.

Make sure that your entire team takes responsibility for documenting meetings, conversations, and especially decisions. Often, a project manager will be responsible for note-taking, but there are tons of meetings and conversations that a busy PM will miss out on. Don't always rely on one person for notes; make note-taking and circulation a shared responsibility. For instance, if you're in a hallway and something interesting or impactful comes up organically in a discussion, don't forget to document it. Taking three to five minutes to share potentially critical info with your team could save you from time and budget worries.

Using a web-based tool to hold all of that information will facilitate good communication and knowledge sharing. Half the battle in the war against poor communications and missed expectations lies in knowing when and where communication should happen and how it will be documented.

Note-Taking Tips

Many of us are terrible note-takers, especially when we're trying to take part in conversations and document them at the same time. If it's possible, have someone join your meeting with the sole purpose of documenting the meeting. If that's not possible (which is completely reasonable), do your best to document what you can. Here are some quick tips for taking useful, actionable meeting notes:

- **Train yourself to listen for keywords and phrases.** Sticking to what's important to the conversation is key.

- **Write notes in your own words.** That's right, you don't need to document the conversation verbatim.

- **Categorize your thoughts by key points, decisions, and action items.** This will help you communicate the most important details and follow up on them. This takes some work, so it might be something you do after the meeting.

- **Use a tool that works best for you and utilize it as much as possible.** For example, some people like the iPhone text expansion feature for quick word recognition and less typing. Others like Evernote for its formatting and filing capabilities. No matter what tool you pick, be sure to familiarize yourself with it and get the most out of it.

- **Share your meeting notes in a place where they can not only be viewed, but also be commented on or edited.** This helps to share the responsibility of the accuracy of your notes. Win-win!

Tactical Tips to Keep Expectations in Check

Setting expectations feels like the easy work once you're knee deep in project land. The tough work comes when you have to keep your expectations in place. You've got to rely on the groundwork laid to get everyone on the same page and follow up on those things regularly. Here are some ways to keep your team in check with project expectations.

1. **Create shared to-do lists.**

   Lists always help to track tasks, milestones, and related deliverables. When your whole team has access, there's never a question about who is doing what and when to expect task completion. You can track subtasks as a team and keep each other in the loop on progress and dependencies.

   After you've got your list documented, make sure that you've clearly assigned responsibilities and check in on them. If you're seeing that a team member is behind, be proactive and comment on it through the shared to-do list. The point of an open list is to make sure that you're all up-to-date on the status of work at all times. A list like this will foster real-time communication, whether that is through in-person discussions, instant messages, or emails. The idea is to work in the open and share progress to build team support. This is the type of activity that helps teams build trust and gain project efficiencies.

2. **Don't worry about delivering bad news.**

   If you think something might go wrong, talk about it. There is no use in keeping worrisome news hidden. Be sure to always keep a "Risks" section in your status report, because the last thing you want to do is surprise a client with news that something is going over budget or past your timeline. At the end of the day, this is business, and if you have the project's best interests in mind, you'll look for and be honest about those risks without question.

   Keeping an eye on those risks can let you anticipate the needs of your team or your client before they even realize they exist. When you do that, you feel like you've won.

3. **Ask questions and listen to responses.**

   Don't be bashful about figuring out what you may not know or understand. Chances are, asking questions will help you and your team sort out expectations related to project requirements, feedback, processes, and even the client's happiness levels. When you hear an answer, don't take it at face value. Think about how it may impact your project and be sure to follow up with more questions (if needed, of course).

by Sam Barnes
Sam Barnes is the engineering manager at Marks and Spencer in the UK. He's also a seasoned digital PM, and partner in Pathfinder DPM, a training company for digital project managers.

I once found myself in the unusual position of running two almost identical projects with the same client and production teams. In effect, it felt like a project management A/B test. I took over project A about three-quarters of the way through and found the client and production teams were really unhappy. The project was sold with a realistic budget, scope, and timeline, so I wondered how it could have all gone so wrong.

After discussion, it became clear that the project-specific problems weren't the root issues. Instead, the team was experiencing issues due to poor expectation setting and management. For months, the clients thought everything was going well until suddenly the project manager asked for additional budget and time. As you might expect, this shocked the client, and he asked why. He received weak reasons that ultimately translated to "digital projects are hard and things happen, sorry." Ouch. Not acceptable.

From that point forward, everyone had a negative experience on the project. The client felt duped and demanded delivery with no additional budget or time, causing stress to the project manager and production team. Realizing it was too late to repair the relationships, I focused on delivery and helped the team get the project finished as quickly as possible.

There is no winner in this scenario. Only through making these mistakes myself did I know there was a better way, but for now I just hoped the experience had not put the client off working with us again. Luckily, it didn't. Three months later, the same client and agency teams had to work on another similar project together (the "B" in this A/B test).

At the kick-off meeting, everyone, including myself, was apprehensive. But this time, I introduced a weekly status report. Would this mean we'd encounter no problems? No, of course not. Would it ensure that we delivered on time, budget, and scope? Nope. But what it would do was minimize the chance of anyone involved not understanding what was happening and why.

So, on the first Friday after the project started, I sent the first weekly report to both the client and production teams. To most, this seemed like a pretty uneventful moment, perhaps even a bit dogmatic, but I knew this was the foundation on which the rest of the project would sit and would demonstrate its power later on.

continues on next page

Did project B encounter issues? Absolutely, but this time everyone knew about them quickly, or by Friday at the very least. Instead of keeping quiet and hoping we could make up the time, problems were openly discussed, and we came to some sensible agreements.

This approach resulted in a more harmonious working relationship and despite the project coming in over budget and a little late, the consensus was that it had gone well. Some people even commented that they'd enjoyed working on it! This rare A/B test showed me the true power of setting and managing expectations and how it can be achieved through very simple methods.

TL; DR

Time is tight, and so is your budget. But you can't get away without doing some of this work to make sure that your team and clients are aligned in order to meet project expectations. Do these things to ensure that you're keeping expectations in check:

- Review your SOW in detail and make sure that you understand it through and through.

- Conduct pre-project kick-off meetings with your team and clients to ensure that everyone understands the following items:

  - Project goals and scope

  - Timeline and dependencies

  - Communication expectations/needs

- Create a weekly status report that communicates the following information:

  - What was done last week?

  - What is being done this week?

  - What is the update on the timeline and budget?

  - What are the project risks or blockers?

- Make time to take meeting notes and share them with your team and clients.

Scope Is Creepin'

*An exercise in paring down scope
at the art supply store.*

My eight-year-old daughter, Juliet, is an artist. I'm amazed by her talent at such a young age, and I want to encourage her to exercise her creativity. Part of that encouragement comes with art supplies. I mean, you can't be inspired to learn about and create great things without the proper tools, right?

She recently got into drawing and shading, and asked if she could get a few new pencils. I was more than happy to take her to the art supply store the next day. She offered up the $45 she got for her birthday. It seemed like a good budget for some supplies. We walked the store for a good 40 minutes before she picked up one pencil. After she chose that, she decided to go back and snag all of the things that caught her eye.

Before I knew it, I was holding $150 worth of art supplies. And it was my fault because I didn't clearly explain that she was nearing—or exceeding—her budget after just three items. We stopped for a minute and laid everything out. I explained to her that what she had picked up was worth about $150, and she had $45. I was happy to add $25 to that so she could get some extra stuff, but she still had to cut $80 worth of supplies. It was not an easy thing to do—I felt like it was my fault. But I couldn't buy it all for her—for so many reasons that any parent would agree with. She wasn't happy, but she was cool about it. We itemized what each cost, and I helped her decide on what she could afford. Thirty minutes later we left the store with $70 worth of supplies.

Managing and Embracing Change

Projects change constantly. Whether a client's business changes, a new stakeholder gets pulled into a project, a team member comes up with a big, new idea, or a piece of functionality just isn't working the way the stakeholders expected, you're going to be forced to have discussions about how to handle that change. These are the things that completely destroy your timelines and tend to upset teams who have worked so hard on something. But most of all, these changes will affect your project scope and potentially drain your budget. Our initial reaction to scope creep—or even just simple change— as humans is to recoil and reject. But with a project run by clients or lofty stakeholders, that's impossible. The best thing you can do is to accept the change, question it, and mold it into something that will make the project a success.

The Devil Is in the Details

The minute you hear about a change, or a request to push the boundaries of your scope, you'll get worried. It's normal. But when you're caught up in the moment, it's always good to remember that you've got a lot to fall back on, provided you've done your due diligence and have truly read and understood your scope, built a plan based on that scope, and have completely vetted it with your team and your clients.

If you have faith in the fact that you've kept your project on track by tying everything back to what's in scope, you'll have an easy time of figuring out what to do with any request for change. When that request does come, don't feel as though you have to accept or deny it immediately. Always feel free to stop a conversation and say, "Let me refer back to the estimate/scope/plan and get back to you." You should never expect to (or be expected to) have every detail committed to memory—especially if you're responsible for more than one project. So take your time, don't jump to provide an immediate answer, and always remember that a solid response is going to have the best impact.

> **NOTE** KEEP YOUR SCOPE CLOSE BY
>
> You'll never remember every detail of your scope. Or your plan. Or any of the documents on your project. Keep a quick link to them so that you—and everyone else on your team—can access them to review at any time.

Keep Your Plan Updated, Save Heartache

The first version of your plan is your baseline, and it outlines every step you need to take to get from the beginning to the end of your project. However, it won't be the last version of your plan either. If you've done this right and put some real thought into your plan, you've based it on your estimate and scope. Sure, plans can change, but referring to that first plan as your baseline will help you in arguing the case for more time or more budget when new scope starts to creep in.

Not every project change will result in a scope change. Sometimes, unexpected things happen: someone gets sick, a stakeholder has gone missing and can't provide feedback, a baby is born! You get the idea. But when your plans do change, make an update and notify everyone involved. Always communicate it in several ways. Here are some helpful strategies for communicating changes.

1. **Provide an updated project plan.**

   Update all impacted tasks and keep notes on extensions in your newest version. For instance, if a client milestone is missed and a deadline is extended, make a note in the planned task. Most planning software includes a handy "notes" field, so it's easy to note, "Baseline date was <month/day/year>. Actual was adjusted in this plan on <month/day/year> due to <silly reason>." After you've updated everything and double-checked your dates, make a new version and save the old one in a safe spot.

2. **Provide an update in a project status report.**

   Always report on your timeline in your project status reports. You can provide a percent-completed update based on what's in your plan. If you want to be really consistent (and you should), replicate the note made in your plan in your status report.

3. **Discuss changes and impacts.**

   A date is a date. If someone misses a deadline, your next delivery date might be impacted as well as the final deadline. Missing deadlines will most often cause an impact, whether it is on your resourcing plan, the next delivery, or the final deadline. Don't fear the conversation about timeline issues and impacts, especially if you've made the time to discuss and review your baseline plan. Talking things out while a change is happening will help everyone to understand what is being affected.

4. **Note or add the change in your project requirements document.**

   This document is created for your team to review/revise and check against throughout the project. Don't forget to refer back to it and keep it up-to-date, since there are times when the document can become buried in the project.

5. **Be open about your change control process.**

   This is equal parts setting expectations and creating processes. If you're in a larger organization, you might be required to complete a series of approvals to ensure that everyone on your team agrees to a change in plans or timeline. On smaller projects with smaller teams, it's often easy to merely take everyone's word for it and keep moving on with the changes. In that instance, it's not a horrible idea to create a "paper trail" associated with a particular conversation or change.

Write a Simple Change Request

Use your judgment here, but it's never a bad thing to write a change request for a non-scope-related change. It can be a good way to cover your bases and ensure that no one will go back on what had been verbally agreed to via email. Any good change request will include the following information:

- Description of the change

- Approach to change

- Schedule/timeline impact

- Risk

- Cost (if applicable)

- Signatures (*always* require these)

Money, Money, Money

People hate talking about money. It's your job to talk about things that people hate. That's just how it is for project managers. The best way to approach topics like budget overages and scope creep is to handle them head-on with a conversation and a change request.

A change in scope should never be a surprise to you or your clients. They wouldn't call it "scope creep" if it didn't slowly slither up on you. Sure, some requests are obviously out of the boundaries of your scope, and you can address them immediately. But there's often that one feature or requirement that starts as a manageable piece of scope and slowly evolves into something else. This, my friends, is *scope creep*. And it's your job to keep an eye on these things and make sure that they are not killing your budget.

Tame the Scope Creep

When you do realize that they're going to kill your budget, use your documentation and status reports to call out the scope creep issue (see Figure 10.1). The first step would be to reassess the budget and note where the work is trending. Take a look at the project hours and estimated effort, and then check in with your team to see if they would estimate an overage. If they confirm, you need to make your clients aware right away. If they think it's fine and you're just being an alarmist, you might want to let your clients know about the potential risk anyway. It never hurts to show that you're thinking ahead and being budget conscious. The best way to do this is to make it formal. Create a "Risk/Issues" section in your status report so that you can write out potential issues and then discuss them with your clients.

FIGURE 10.1

Beware the scope creep. He's not an actual guy, but sometimes he manifests himself in ideas, conversations, and actual work. He's around...and he's out to get your time and money!

Discussing the issue might feel uncomfortable, but it doesn't have to be. Calling things out early will give you the time to think through a mitigation plan and discuss it with your clients. Plus, by not waiting until the very last minute to call out the issue, you're positioning it in a way that will help everyone involved to devise a reasonable approach to the change; you always have your scope and timeline to back you up. A well-researched and planned discussion surrounding the risk of scope creep will help put you, your client, and the potential issue at ease. Anything can be sorted out with planning and discussion.

When a Change in Scope Is Not Acceptable

Sometimes you'll get to a point where the team can't continue work without a budgetary change request, but the clients don't want to agree to it. Talk about uncomfortable! It's never easy to proceed under these conditions, but as the PM, you have to come up with options. Here are a few scenarios to think through:

- Can you trade scope? Meaning, if your team does let scope creep commit a hostile takeover, can you cut something else from the project to make up for lost time and/or budget?

- How will the change impact the quality of the product? If it's going to make it worse, how does that impact your bottom line?

- Is your company willing to "eat" some of the cost in order to develop a better product and keep the clients happy? If yes, what is that cost?

No matter what the answer is, you'll need the buy-in of your team and management to make the change that is best for your project, your clients, and your company. It's never an easy decision to make.

Don't Forsake Quality

At the end of the day, everyone wants to deliver a quality product that is successful and evokes a sense of pride. While it's important to complete and deliver on time and under budget, you should never lose sight of delivering a quality product; the expectations of what you're to deliver should never be overshadowed by the scope or timeline. You'll always use your timeline and budget as the guiding light, but it's important to set forth what will make the project a success in the eyes of your clients and your team. Just a few questions, asked at the beginning of a project can help establish an agreement on what success looks like to everyone involved.

- What are the goals of the project?
- What will make the project a success?
- What can we do to ensure success?
- How will we measure success after completion of the project?

Asking these questions will allow your team to set some targets within the context of your project budget and timeline. Having goals sets the stage for how you can meet them within the constraints of the project. Goals can also enable you to gauge the validity of new requests as they come in. If you're experiencing scope creep and the work doesn't actually meet a goal, it's much easier to cut it out.

It's Not Easy, and It's Not Scary Either

A good project manager can sense scope creep the minute it's hinted at. A better project manager takes the time to diagnose the scope creep, study it, and develop an approach to accept or deny it. The best project managers take the time to get through all of those steps and approach the situation with a level head. Any project problem—scope related or not—can be resolved with a conversation that references previous work you've done on your project. In fact, all of the time you put into creating an estimate, scope, and timeline will make approaching any problem easier.

Defending Your Scope

by Rachel Gertz
Rachel Gertz, cofounder of Louder Than Ten, is training the
next generation of digital project managers.

"I have a really good idea. Can we just add a giant pop-up with a monster on the screen and when it jumps out on the home page, it can introduce our services? It'll be, like, really interactive." We were well into our final app design review with a client, and monsters were not part of our scope.

Clients have ideas. Lots of them. Some of them are good, some not so much. This is how I handled one particular client idea while PMing and doing content strategy for a web project: First, I watched for the scope creep words: can we, just, add, adjust, move, but, a little. These types of words reek of scope creep. If you see them, be prepared to fine-tune your PM nose. Tune up your goals.

One of the key things I've learned as a PM is that everything you do needs to tie back to what the organization wants to do—their business goals—not just the project's goals. This keeps the project and every deliverable focused on reinforcing those goals. It also gives you a strong business case for why a certain path might hurt the project or the company. Scope increases aren't bad unless they sneak by you or derail your direction. So I told the client that the idea sounded interesting, but that we'd have to revisit their goals to increase revenue and have a customer-friendly interface to see if this monster idea lined up with those. Of course, it didn't, and I introduced some other ideas that we could schedule and scope together, but the client held fast. She still wanted her monster.

When clients have ideas they share with you, you've got to be sensitive about how you respond. They make themselves vulnerable when they express themselves and if you're not careful, shutting them down directly without context can hurt them or your relationship. Your client is really just you in a mirror—you want the same things. Not all your ideas are good either, but a tactful response is worth the uncomfortable conversation it will take to clarify both of your wants. I told the client that the idea didn't fit with their goals and that the distracting experience would potentially lose them money, and then I finished up with a solemn: "We just wouldn't feel good about doing that and couldn't stand behind our work. What else can we do to accomplish what you're after? We'd be happy to test some things if you can put aside some extra budget." Instead of shutting her down or ridiculing her idea, I made sure to communicate that it was now going to impact the work we could do and that we weren't prepared to do it, but were willing to try other things. A soft "no."

After a couple conversations around the goals of the page and company, and some gentle but firm guidance, the client and I nixed the monster idea and continued our development schedule without a hitch.

TL; DR

There is no denying change when it comes to digital projects. A number of things can happen to test the boundaries of your scope and timeline. Your best bet to handle or adapt to these changes is to embrace them and do these things:

- Ensure that your plan is based on the reality that is your project scope.

- When a change does occur, update your project documentation and communicate the change to everyone involved. This will ensure that everyone is aware and not ignoring the issue.

- If you've got to increase your budget for a change, talk about it and document it.

- You don't always have to accept a full change. Talk through options of how you might make something happen without fully increasing your scope. Remember, projects are partnerships.

- Don't ever forsake the quality of your project for a change. Keep your project goals in mind because they could help you rule out an impending change.

Facilitation
for PMs

*Helping shoppers can actually develop
great facilitation skills.*

I worked in retail when I was a teenager. Yup, I was a mall rat for a summer or two. I sold expensive sunglasses. Looking back on the experience, I can say that it gave me the perspective to understand how people make decisions when spending a lot of money on an item that they could get for much cheaper elsewhere. It was interesting to see what would drive someone to make a final decision to purchase a $200+ pair of sunglasses. As the salesman, I was incented to make sales for a commission. But I was also paid a base hourly wage, so I wasn't a viper. I like to think I helped people make decisions on their purchases.

I remember a time when a couple came into the store and told me they were looking to purchase a gift for a family member. I asked them what styles they were looking for and gave them some options. We started with five pairs of sunglasses, and they narrowed it down to two options. They discussed the merit of the two (very similar) styles for what felt like four hours. Because I wanted to make the sale, but I didn't know the person who was to receive the gift, I did everything in my power to help—without being that annoying sales-person. I shared facts about the glasses: lens colors, weights, quality, return policy, etc. I also asked them things like, "When do you picture her wearing these?" and "What is her style?" Lots of ridiculous questions that I couldn't believe were coming out of my mouth. Personally, I didn't like either style. But I would never tell them that!

Eventually, they made a decision that they both agreed on and were happy about it. While I was processing the credit card, they thanked me for the help because I helped them make a decision. All I could think was, "Sure, great. I just hope she doesn't come back next week to return them!" Thankfully, that never happened. And it helped me understand what actually helped my customers to make a purchasing decision. I was able to use that experience to sell more and eventually to assist other people outside of the store to make decisions that felt right for them—not just for me.

People Make Projects Difficult

It's not the technology or the creativity—it's the people who produce the ideas and make the final decisions. Often, a project manager's role becomes that of a facilitator, because part of keeping a project on track is keeping the people on track. That doesn't mean forcing decisions, but maybe gently suggesting ways to arrive at decisions. That's right, it's part process and *all* human, because effectively managing people and their interactions is part of managing the project.

Effective project management doesn't happen without good facilitation skills. Project success depends on how the team is facilitated to make decisions, solve problems, and respond to risks and changes. PM facilitation provides a foundation of organization that allows a team to be creative and explore options together, but also make decisions, perform at a highly functioning level, and deliver on specific outcomes.

As a project manager, you walk the line between managing and intervening to make sure that work progresses with efficiency and stability. Essentially, you want to be an active member of the team, and that is done through facilitating the best decisions for the success of the project.

Brush Up Your Facilitation Skills

What does it take to be a great project facilitator while also being a project manager? In a perfect world, you would have a person who could act as just a facilitator—looking from the outside in to ask questions, challenge ideas, resolve disagreements, and generally help the team progress. In reality, that work typically falls on the shoulders of the project manager. And it's no easy feat. Do you have what it takes to do the job? Sure you do, especially if you think about it in terms of what a facilitator might do. For instance, you might have to do the following:

- Understand your team, their relationships, and the way they work together.

- Keep an eye on project goals and how decisions being made might meet them.

- Analyze and understand team issues and conflicts.

- Recommend techniques or tools to sustain project momentum.

- Manage team meetings effectively.

- Ensure that the team is always making the best use of time.

- Champion effective communications.

That's a lot to keep an eye on, particularly when you're also responsible for managing the process, to-do lists, a budget, scope, and maybe even project stakeholders. No matter what you do, it will be difficult to manage your own time and the project, its process, the team, and its decisions. Think you're up to it? Yes, you are. If you're feeling hesitant, or even a little confused, here are some core values to guide you when taking on the facilitation role.

Be Neutral

You want to deliver a successful project, and to you, success is rooted in meeting project goals. Don't get wrapped up in the end result. We've all got opinions, particularly when it comes to how something looks. But that is not your role on the project. Put your personal opinion aside and focus on what will get you to the desired result rather than the result itself.

Keep Planning

Project plans are great because they show you the long-term trajectory of a project. But you should know that every decision, meeting, or task might require its own plan to ensure success. As a PM facilitator, you've got to have a plan for how your team will arrive most effectively at a conversation, decision, or deliverable. It's your job to plan that.

Be Energetic

The best way to lead teams to decisions is by motivating them with an energy that inspires a positive outcome. If you're sitting on the sidelines just watching or keeping quiet, then you're doing it incorrectly. When you put a plan in place and you have faith in it, you can facilitate with an energy that will inspire action. It's one of those magical parts of great project management that is truly hard to define. If you just be yourself and do everything you can to motivate a team, you will absolutely see results (and people will see that you helped in a major way).

Be a Great Communicator

Not to beat a dead horse, but a good PM doesn't happen without great communication skills, and good facilitation can't exist without effective communications. As a project facilitator, you will contribute to your team reaching mutual understanding of project goals and the best path to meet them. How do you do that? You pay special attention to each individual and how they are contributing to the process and the project, and make sure that their opinion is not only heard, but valued. When times are difficult, you do everything you can to understand each point of view and ensure that all options are being considered. Sometimes, you'll act as a translator; sometimes, you'll be a mediator; and at all times, you'll be a friend and confidant to the whole team.

Be an Authority

Someone on the team has to set the boundaries for how you will work, how long something should take, and when a conversation has to stop. You'll find yourself in conversations that go round and round, and it feels like there is no end. As a facilitator, you need to step in, set (or even reset) boundaries, and do everything in your power to get a conversation back on track. Remember, keep the goals in mind, and you'll have a great filter for how to resolve any scenario.

> **NOTE** THE VOICE OF REASON
>
> Don't be afraid to speak up! You may not be the final decision maker, but you are there to keep things on track, and sometimes that final decision maker needs your help to set boundaries.

Facilitation Techniques

Anyone can host a meeting, run a brainstorming session, or collect ideas from a team, but not everyone can do it efficiently. It takes the right balance and knowledge of project goals, team expertise, timing, tools, and you guessed it, facilitation skills. Before you jump in to a meeting, be sure to think about what will make for a great session:

Be Prepared

If you want to get the most out of your session, then prepare yourself and your team for the session. This might mean that you have to spend some time thinking about how the meeting will flow, what you will present, or what questions you will ask the team in order to ignite conversation and debate. Alternately, if you need someone else on the team to take some responsibility, make sure that you give that person time to prepare as well. After all, there is nothing worse than attending a meeting that feels disorganized.

Create the Right Environment

Meeting space comes at a premium in many offices. In order to run an effective session, make sure that the work you do will be accommodated by the space you have. Think about it. Will you need the following?

- Whiteboards

- Group seating

- Wall space

- Flip charts, sticky notes, markers

- Technology set up for remote attendees to see/participate

- Round tables with seats

- One large table

The more you have prepared in terms of space and materials, the better the environment will be. And the more excited your team will be to participate.

> **NOTE** REMOTE MEETINGS
>
> If you're running a remote meeting or session, get into your meeting room 10–15 minutes in advance of the meeting to get the technology sorted out so that you can start without any delays. These sessions can often take longer than in-person sessions because of communication challenges. This is something to consider when scheduling and planning your agenda.

Ensure That the Expected Outcomes or Objectives Are Clear

Set an agenda that includes a statement of meeting goals. At the top of the meeting, be sure to review these goals with the group. You may even want to discuss what meeting these goals will mean to the rest of the project. Setting context can help to keep everyone on track.

Establish Expectations

Your agenda and meeting goals will set expectations for the meetings. At the same time, try to set some ground rules for your meeting. For instance, if you have limited time, you might agree that any mention of an outside topic will be shut down by the facilitator and added to a list of things to discuss later.

Your facilitation style needs to meet the needs of the group and the goals for the meeting. For example, you may want to facilitate by stepping back and letting conversation take place so that you can witness interactions and record decisions. Or you may lead a group exercise to see outcomes and discuss them as a group. No matter what, you have to recognize that a "one-size-fits-all" approach to facilitating meetings does not work.

Helpful Facilitation Tools

There are plenty of ways to engage a team, lead them to healthy conversations, and even make decisions. Some are simple conversational tactics, while others are interactive activities. You'll do what feels right based on the goals and people involved. Here are a few that can help you.

Gate Keeping

The loudest voice can't win! Everyone on a project should have equal footing when it comes to collaboration and discussion. With gate-keeping, all participants have an equal opportunity to influence the decision to be made. As a facilitator, you can help make this happen by gate opening and gate closing.

- **Gate opening:** There's always a quiet team member who tends to sit back and speak less or not speak at all. The problem is, that person may have information and thoughts that could impact decisions, or better yet, help make them. As the facilitator, it's your job to get those people talking. Open the gate by asking direct questions of that person. Engage them with the group. You might be putting them on the spot, but it's important to do when you want a well-rounded, inclusive conversation.

- **Gate closing:** Don't let one person dominate a conversation or meeting, because when you do, you will end up with annoyed team members who are less motivated to act on ideas. It's simple: inclusion builds trust, motivates teams, and helps decisions to be made. So, if John is dominating a meeting, simply interrupt him and ask if anyone else has a perspective to add. It might feel awkward, but your team will thank you for it later (and, you'll get a better conversation going).

Use Flip Charts, Post-it Notes, and Sharpies

Sounds like an endorsement of specific merchandise in office supply stores, huh? Well, it kind of is (see Figure 11.1)! It's amazing how much our highly technical teams use paper to generate ideas and consensus. But providing a hands-on experience allows all participants to provide ideas or input (bonus points for those shy people who'd rather write than speak), discuss them, merge them, and even come up with visual ways to represent complex ideas.

FIGURE 11.1
Ironically, the digital industry seems to be keeping 3M in business.

> **NOTE** BETTER MEETING INTERACTION BY DESIGN
>
> Want some ideas for exercises to run? Check out *Gamestorming* by Dave Gray, Sunni Brown, and James Macanufo. It includes several group activities, exercises, and games that help generate ideas and even build consensus.

Brainstorm

We all conduct brainstorming sessions with the intent of generating as many ideas as possible, but are they always effective? Probably not. If you're going to conduct a brainstorming session, you should structure that meeting and set some basic ground rules. If you truly want to create an environment that is accepting, open, and ready to be creative, remind everyone of the following tenets:

- There is no such thing as a bad idea.

- Good ideas can come from anyone on a team.

- The goal of the meeting is to get as many ideas out as possible.

- You'll discuss the merits of all ideas as a group.

- You'll refine the list of ideas and remove the ones that just won't work.

- There are no hard feelings if your idea is not selected.

- You will end the session with at least one final idea.

Clustering

Need to get an answer to a complex question or gain consensus on a topic or issue? You can get your team to come to a decision quickly with a clustering exercise. There are a number of ways to do this, but you can start with this technique.

Pose the question/topic/scenario and have each attendee record their responses on Post-it Notes (one response per note). Then have meeting participants quickly place the stickies into groups. Again, they make the decision and do the work. You can step back to facilitate the process, watch for emergent themes/outcomes, and then question the final results. This approach should lead to productive conversation with the goal of making a decision. This kind of exercise can be very helpful when you're trying to diagnose an issue or a pain point, generate ideas, gain feedback, and much more. Plus, it's a quick and easy way to get anything and everything on the table (or wall).

The "T"

The "T" is a focusing technique that can put an end to what may feel like a never-ending unstructured debate. At the same time, it can help your team come to a decision with confidence and ease.

Here's what to do: Draw a "T" for each item under debate on a white-board or flipchart; then have the group brainstorm and record the pros and cons (again, one point per sticky note). When they are done recording, they will place their points on the "T." From there, you will begin to see emergent themes, which will show consensus or allow for further debate, which is a discussion that you will facilitate. This exercise is really great for figuring out issues or discussion points that stand in the way of a decision (see Figure 11.2).

FIGURE 11.2
Use the "T" when you need to get consensus—or discussion about issues—quickly. You can write directly on a board or have participants write responses on sticky notes and then cluster them.

Beat Meeting Fatigue

Every project manager's day is filled with meetings. These can be meetings about projects, meetings with clients, ad hoc team gatherings, internal and client status meetings, and so on. The list of possibilities for work gatherings seems endless. That can be a problem! Too many meetings can mean lower team productivity, and too few meetings can cause strains in team communication and gaps in knowledge. There's certainly a tricky balance to find the right amount of meeting time, and it's tough to ensure that each one will be productive.

Finding the right balance and offering the team value in each and every meeting often lies on a project manager's shoulders. But don't worry, you can become a PM meeting master by finding the balance between the "art" of communicating a meeting's importance and the "science" of how it's best managed.

First Step: Determine Meeting Value

Of course, there is no mystery in what makes a meeting successful or abysmally bad. Just scheduling a meeting can be difficult, what with ensuring timeliness of the discussion, navigating the issues at hand, and coordinating people (and their busy schedules). Plus, you have to deal with internal factors. For instance, in some organizational cultures, meetings are seen as unnecessary or bad. In others, they are healthy places to exchange ideas, or even to get work done. Whether you think they're good or a hassle, you should know that you, the project manager, can help determine the time, length, agenda, and value of a meeting.

Before you "throw something on the calendar," it's best to think strategically about your meeting. Part of the reason many professionals sigh or grunt at the thought of a meeting is because it could be seen as an interruption in their day. Think about it—if you're working with a team who is making a product, they need a good amount of time to sit down and focus on what they're making. A meeting about something peripheral to the project can throw their concentration off very quickly. So how can you determine if a meeting is actually needed? Follow these guidelines:

1. **Be clear about the meeting's goals.**

   It may seem silly, but going into a meeting knowing what you want to get out of it will help you make decisions on who should be there, when it should happen, and how long it might take. Before you schedule anything, ask yourself, "What is the goal of this meeting?" and "Do we actually need a meeting to hit this goal?"

2. **Who needs to be in this meeting?**

   Look back at that goal. Is it something that your entire team should be involved in? Be sure to protect your time as well as your team's time. The last thing you want to do is pull people into a meeting if they are not needed. Think about it this way: "Will this person talk in the meeting?" If the answer is "no," he is off the hook.

3. **What is needed to make this meeting a success?**

   Give attendees everything they will need for this meeting in advance. Your best bet is to attach the information to the meeting invitation. This could include advance notes, handouts, documents for review, etc. The more prep you can provide, the more productive the meeting will be.

4. **Does this meeting have to happen today, tomorrow, or even next week?**

   Think back to that meeting goal. How will it impact your project, decisions that are being made, the people in the meeting (and the work they have going on), your clients, your budget, and timeline? There's a lot in play there! Project managers often think every issue is the most important, but when it comes to determining the best timing—or if a meeting can wait—take the time to think through those impacts and create priorities.

5. **How much time do we need?**

   Again, protect that time! If you only need 15 minutes, take it. If you need an hour and a half, that's OK, too. Be sure to communicate the intent and value of the meeting to attendees so they come into it knowing that you're not wasting their time. Remember, you are the PM, and you control the calendar. If a meeting will stress your calendar or your team's, you can take responsibility for finding a better time.

6. **What is the agenda?**

   Always create a meeting agenda, even for the shortest meetings. Be sure to include the meeting agenda in the meeting invitation and add names next to conversation or presentation points so that attendees know their responsibility for the meeting. Having an agenda will help you stick to the meeting goals, formulate what potential to-do items could be, and keep the conversation on track.

   NOTE COURTEOUS SCHEDULING

   Never double-book someone for a meeting. If someone is unable to make a meeting and you can't find another time, approach that person and ask if they are OK with missing the meeting. Promise thorough meeting notes and offer a follow-up if you just need to make a meeting happen and that person is secondary to the conversation at hand.

Want to save yourself time? Set a team rule: No meetings should be scheduled without an agenda. After all, if you don't know what a meeting is about or for, why attend? You deserve to know that, as well as to have the space and time to prepare.

Ensure Meeting Greatness

After you've determined that your meeting will happen and you've set the agenda, it's up to you to make sure that it lives up to everyone's expectations. Remember, you are the project facilitator, so it is absolutely your job. No fear, you can do this! You can lay the groundwork for a highly productive meeting by establishing some rules, creating some roles, and addressing potential distractions.

Determine Meeting Roles

If your meeting is fairly formal, make sure that you have some basic roles and responsibilities covered. Read through the following roles and determine what's right for you and the people you're gathering.

- **Leader:** The leader is the team member who calls the meeting and takes responsibility for communication before and after. In addition to being a participant, this person may guide discussion on all items or perhaps ask others to lead the entirety (or parts) of the meeting.

- **Facilitator:** The facilitator keeps the discussion and decision-making process moving along. Typically, the facilitator is not involved in the content of the meeting—rather, they guide conversation through the agenda and help the group with decision-making.

- **Recorder:** The note-taker is a non-negotiable role in any meeting. Meeting notes are very important. Having someone record general points made, action items, and to-dos is critical to the success of any meeting. On that note, meeting notes should be distributed as soon after the meeting as possible. It can be very helpful to store notes in a system where meeting attendees can review and update points made.

- **Timekeeper:** If you want to be really expedient, ask someone to keep an eye on the clock. Start on time and end on time, and everyone will be happy.

These roles are only meant to be general guidelines. Not every meeting will even have enough attendees to make this happen! A general rule of thumb should be that the folks whose attendance is critical to the conversation at hand are in attendance with no additional "job" in the meeting. If you need help with moderation or note-taking, by all means, ask for help. After all, you're a PM, not Superman.

Make It a Productive Meeting

All too often, attendees will show up with a laptop or devices in tow. It's really hard to disconnect these days, but if the people meant to be engaged in the discussion are sidetracked by what's happening on their screens, they will be distracted from your important conversation. If you're feeling brave, ask attendees to leave laptops and devices on their desks.

At the end of the day, it's your job as a PM and facilitator to make sure that the team stays on task and that the goals of your meeting are met. Maybe you'll employ an exercise or facilitate a conversation, or maybe you'll sit back and record results. But no matter what you do, make sure that you're not wasting anyone's time.

by Sara Wachter-Boettcher
Content strategy consultant, author of Content Everywhere *and*
co-author of Design for Real Life

I started doing content strategy work because I kept seeing clients with the same problems: overwhelming navigation, big blobs of inconsistent copy, and pages and pages of fluff that didn't need to be there. So I set out to fix them: audit the content, rewrite the copy, reorganize the site around a new information architecture. I was pretty good at it, too.

Eventually, I found myself working with a large government agency with thousands of pages of content—and I was excited to whip that site into shape. I built content models, established style guidelines, and edited my heart out. By launch, I had transformed their mess into something I was proud of.

It didn't last. Pretty soon, the copy grew back into a blob. People stopped following the style guide. Critical CMS fields were left empty.

What I realized is that my content expertise wasn't cutting it. I also needed to bring people along with me—people who might not be web experts, but who would be responsible for sustaining things after I'd gone. That's when I found facilitation.

Rather than trying to control the content myself, I learned to focus on helping teams see their content differently, build skills, and make content choices themselves. It's a skill I've been honing for several years now, and it's completely changed how I work.

For example, I recently had another client with thousands of pages of content cluttering a dated, hard-to-use website. This time, I didn't jump into "fix" mode. Instead, I invited everyone who had a stake in the site to help make content decisions, right from the start.

In our first major workshop, when we were deciding what was most important to communicate, I facilitated an activity that used mad libs—a simple fill-in-the-blank statement about the website's goals and audience that the team had to collaborate on and come up with a plan they could all agree to. This gave people who often didn't feel like they had a say, a chance to be included and heard, and it also forced everyone to forget their pet projects and focus on what really mattered. Everyone left the workshop with a core understanding of what we were trying to do—and a tool they could use later to keep the content on track.

Later on, we needed to determine how the existing content needed to adapt for the new strategy. Rather than *me* telling them what to fix, I instead facilitated an audit workshop, where the people who owned the content looked at pages together and assessed them using the strategy they'd all agreed on. This made the strategy click—taking it from an abstract concept to something that would drive even tiny writing decisions. That never would have happened if I'd done it for them.

The results weren't perfect, of course. The team still ended up with a little more jargon and a little longer copy than I would have liked. That's OK. They made progress—and when their website launched, they had the skills and habits to keep it on track.

TL; DR

Understand what it means to be a facilitator: Set the tone for conversations. Allow for the space and time that projects require for work to be done and decisions to be made. Often, people and their opinions get in the way of those things being done in a timely fashion. It's the PM's job to facilitate the conversations and process that lead teams to wrap up projects successfully. Here's how to do it:

- Decisions, plan for the best ways to meet them.

- Remember, you have to be the PM, not a critic. Stay neutral and help teams to achieve consensus.

- Be authoritative. Lead a process that helps your team make decisions. Step in when they need to be reeled in, because your team needs you to keep them on track.

- Set the tone and make sure that the environment is conducive to making decisions.

- Always work through the lens of project goals and remind your team of them as needed.

- Build your facilitator's toolkit so that you can use techniques that will generate ideas, build consensus, and lead to decision-making.

- Understand the value of meetings and how to run them effectively without wasting precious work time.

On and Up

I won't indulge you here with another personal story that relates to endings. Rather, I'll tell you that this is just the beginning for elevating digital project management in the industry as well as with traditional project management. We've only begun to explore the best ways to work as digital teams, and I expect more to be introduced and uncovered in the future.

This book serves as a foundation for how to handle any project with any team successfully, even under the most frustrating circumstances. Trust me, I've been there, and I wish I had thought through some of these principles and practices before jumping into those fires. But I never would have been able to correct my mistakes and formulate better practices without making those mistakes. And I urge you to do the same.

Share your experience and practices with those around you. Build upon the principles and practices shared in this book. Have the confidence to lead, facilitate healthy communications, craft processes that work, and be a human who can make mistakes—and recover from them. You can do this.

INDEX

documentation

  communications plan, 161–162

  of conversations, sharing notes, 164–165

  expectations in kick-off meeting, 120

  note-taking in meetings, recorder role, 194

  note-taking tips, 165

  project plans. *See* project plans

  requirements document, 155, 157–160, 173

  scope of work, 152–153, 172–173

  status reports. *See* status reports

E

eagle eye of project manager, 7

empathy of project manager, 7–8

estimates, project, 37–63

  for Agile-ish projects, 55–59

  Agile projects, tasks for, 60–62

  creation of, by project manager, 10

  dictionary definition, 40

  historical data, 45–46

  learn your industry, 41

  need to know, ask questions, 47

  pertinent details, 46

  process, understanding what works, 44–45

  reasons to estimate, 40–41

  roles of people on your team, 42–44

  time and materials vs. fixed fee, 48

  work breakdown structure, 49–54

Event Chain Methodology (ECM), 29

executive stakeholders, 73

expectations, 149–168

  assign project roles with RACI matrix, 156–157

build a communications plan, 161–162

  of communications, 120

  conduct status meetings, 162–164

  in difficult conversations, 141

  document requirements, 157–160

  managing, 161–166

  pre-kick-off meetings, 154–156

  set before project begins, 152

  set with status reports (anecdote), 167–168

  take notes, 164–165

  tips to keep in check, 165–166

  understand the scope, 152–154

Extreme Programming (XP), 28

Extreme Project Management (XPM), 29

F

facilitation, 181–199

  determine meeting roles, 194–195

  make meetings productive, 195

  managing people, 183–184

  skills for, 184–185

  techniques, 186–194

  through activities (anecdote), 196–197

facilitator role in meetings, 194

fixed fee for estimate, 48

flexibility of project manager, 8

flip charts in meetings, 189

front-end developer role, 43

G

Gamestorming (Gray, Brown, and Macanufo), 189

Gantt chart, 92, 95

project plans (*continued*)

  project manager creation and
    managing of, 11

  readability of, 96–97

  sample project and plan, 104–105

  sketches, 87–90

  team review, 97–99

  update for scope changes, 172–173

  using a work breakdown structure,
    91–92

project requirements documentation,
  155, 157–160, 173

projects, getting to know, 65–82

  begin with research, 68–69

  defining working relationships
    (anecdote), 80–81

  know your clients, 76–77

  players, identifying, 71–73

  questions to ask, 70

  red flags, 76–79

  stakeholder decision matrix, 74, 75

  stakeholder interviews, 69–71

  talk about the work, 75–76

pros and cons in the "T," as facilitation
  tool, 190–191

Q

QA tester role, 44

quality and change in scope, 176–177

questions

  asking, and communication, 123

  to choose a methodology, 31–32

  details for estimates, 46–47

  getting to know your project, 70

  in requirements document, 158

R

RACI matrix, assigning project roles,
  156–157

recorder role in meetings, 194

red flags, 76, 77–79, 126

remote meetings, 187

request for change, 172.
    See also scope of work

requirements documentation,
  155, 157–160, 173

research to understand project,
  68–69

researcher role, 43

resource management, 107–114

  burnout, 112–113

  matching people skills to projects,
    111–112

  planning team availability, 109–111

  stakeholders as resources, 113–114

responsible role in RACI matrix, 157

risk

  multiple owners of project, 76

  section for issues and bad news
    in status report, 164, 166,
    174–175

S

sales conundrum, 154

sample work to show, 75

scope creep, defined, 174

scope of work (SOW), 169–180

  and budget, 174, 176

  defending (anecdote), 178–179

  documentation, 152–154, 172–173

  managing change, 169–174

  monitoring, as project manager's
    task, 14

ACKNOWLEDGMENTS

I wrote a book! It took a lot of hard work on nights and weekends, but I made it happen. The thing is, it wouldn't have happened without the support, encouragement and guidance of these people: My wife Emily, who gave me the time I needed in solitude to think, plan, and write. My daughters, Juliet and Sylvie, who inspire me to do more, be better. My family, who probably won't read this book, but are still proud. The folks at Happy Cog, who pushed me to be a better PM and supported me in this weird journey of writing and speaking about a topic that no one else was really talking about. My friends at TeamGantt, who pushed me to write a guide that inspired a book. The fine folks who contributed stories to this book and rallied around the process of writing this book: Sam Barnes, Holly Davis, Sara Wachter-Boettcher, Dave Prior, Rachel Gertz, and Elizabeth Harrin. The people who were kind enough to review the book and provide valuable feedback: Tera Simon, Aaron Irizarry, Dave Garrett, Greg Storey, Sam Kapilia, Trish Tchume, and Cecily Storey, who helped me with all of my formatting issues (MS Word? Not my thing.). And the folks who generously read the book and provided kind words: Karen McGrane, Carl Smith, Ahava Leibtag, and Alison Wagner.

Lastly, to anyone who has read this book: I hope it provides you with the information you need to lead well and be successful. I recognize it takes a village to make a great project happen. I'm grateful for having such a talented, respected, and caring village. Thank you.

ABOUT THE AUTHOR

 **Brett Harned** is a digital project management consultant, coach, and community advocate from Philadelphia, PA. His work focuses on solving issues that are important to organizations that want to produce quality digital projects in harmony. He loves to build processes and communication tactics that work not only for projects, but also for the people involved in them. He works with product companies, digital agencies, and in-house teams with a variety of processes, talents, goals, and challenges. Prior to starting his consultancy, Brett was vice president of project management at Happy Cog, where he mentored a team of PMs and managed projects for companies like Zappos, MTV, and Monotype.

Brett began blogging about his adventures in project management at brettharned.com when he realized that there was a void in the industry for people in the digital PM role. Since then, he has had the privilege to speak at various events internationally and has written for widely read industry websites and publications. He also founded and curates the Digital PM Summit, an annual conference with a focus on supporting a community that leads digital projects.

When he's not wrangling processes and people, Brett likes to discover new music, experiment with photography, and explore the City of Brotherly Love with his wife, two daughters, and their French bulldog.